John N. Smith
Caldecott
RUTLAND.
1981.

RAIDERS OVERHEAD

RAIDERS OVERHEAD

A diary of the London blitz

by Barbara Nixon

Scolar/Gulliver

Scolar Press
90/91 Great Russell Street
London WC1

in association with

Gulliver Publishing Co Ltd
White Lion Walk
Banbury
Oxfordshire
OX16 8UD

British Library Cataloguing in Publication Data

Nixon, Barbara
    Raiders overhead. – Revised and enlarged ed.
    1. London – Bombardment, 1940
    2. London. East End
    3. World War, 1939–1945 – Aerial operations,
    German
    I. Title
    940.54′21′0924   DA760.8.L7

    ISBN 0–906428–06–8

Raiders Overhead text © Barbara Nixon 1980
Barbara Nixon's illustrations © Barbara Nixon 1980

Designed by Nicholas Maddren
Edited and produced by Ian Grant

Frontispiece: Barbara Nixon in 1943

Text set in 11/12 pt Baskerville by Tadd Graphics
Printed and bound in Great Britain by Biddles of Guildford

Contents

Terminology

Air Raid Warnings

'Yellow'	Standby warning
'Red'	Air raid warning
'White'	All clear
'Control'	Report Centre of the Local Authority

Glossary

AFS	Auxiliary Fire Service
ATS	Auxiliary Training Service (later the Women's Royal Army Corps)
BDS	Bomb Disposal Squad
CD	Civil Defence
EC	Emergency Committee
FAP	First Aid Post
HE	High explosive bomb
HRS	Heavy Rescue Service
IB	Incendiary bomb
Incident	Damage caused by one or more bombs
IO	Incident Officer
LCC	London County Council
MI	Major Incident
MO	Medical Officer
SP	Stretcher Party
UXB	Unexploded bomb
WVS	Women's Voluntary Service

The borough was divided into a number of wardens' post areas, according to the population, and each of these areas was sub-divided into sectors.

6

Author's note

During the war, one was not supposed to say where any bomb had dropped – it could be 'helping the enemy' – so I camouflaged the area I was concerned with by saying it was near the river, which, of course, could not be disguised. My borough was Finsbury which now, in all the modern re-organisation and aggrandisement, has been swallowed up in Islington to the north. But in those days it stretched from near Liverpool Street due westwards to Smithfield, covered the area north up King's Cross Road and back along Pentonville and City Roads to include Moorgate and Finsbury Square.

The first eleven chapters of this book were published in 1943. It sold out very quickly (almost any book did in those days) but the paper rationing made it impossible to reprint it. Since now Gulliver Publishing Company so agreeably wish to republish it, I have added a postscript, continuing the story to the end of the war.

April 1980

1

Before the Storm

I JOINED the Wardens' Service because it seemed to me to be the most active and obviously helpful Civil Defence occupation open to women. My own work closed down on the eve of the war; and all that the various organisations, which existed for 'placing' normally intelligent women could do, was to assure me that if only I would leave my name on their lists a little longer, there would presently be a great demand for women of my age, education, and experience.

I wanted an active job; I particularly wanted to avoid being in the position of many women in the First World War—of urging other people to do work they wouldn't think of doing themselves. At that time, the ATS seemed to be mainly a matter of cooking and cleaning, for neither of which was I either competent or inclined; I found that the AFS entailed mainly switch-room work, and First Aid Posts seemed to me to be too reminiscent of Job waiting patiently for troubles to be brought to him.

So in May 1940 I became a voluntary (part-time) warden. I had missed the nervous excitement of the early months of the war, when for hours on end wardens patrolled the streets even more conscientiously than the police, bulky and sweating in full gas equipment, their oilskins scraping and rustling as they shuffled along expecting a gas attack at any moment. By the time that I joined, the public was already grumbling that the full-time Civil Defence personnel were a waste of money—a set of slackers, after easy jobs. Raids at some time, however, were a certainty, unless this country perpetrated a more despicable betrayal of its democratic principles than the rulers of France, and I was not deterred.

I was given a tin hat, a whistle, and a CD respirator. The Post Warden one afternoon conducted me on a tour of the seventeen public shelters in the area. By observation I inferred that wardens kept the paraffin lamps in shelters alight, held the keys of them, and were, in an undefined manner, generally rather responsible for them. But the manner was very undefined. (Several weeks after raids had started, we were forbidden to visit shelters owing to a quarrel that was then in progress between the local Chief Warden and the Chief Shelter Marshal!) I gathered that a warden's main duty was to report any bombs which fell in his area.

The Post itself was in a basement of an old house. It was not strengthened in any way, but across the road was a sunk concrete pill-box, which, later, gave good proof of its strength. When 'yellow' stand-by warnings or alerts sounded, the Post Warden, or his Deputy, a messenger, and one or two other wardens moved over there, while the rest of us went off to our various sectors. The Post area was divided into six or seven of these.

Our chief concern in those days was the black-out. Many of the public were apt to be contumacious about their lights, until bombing started. Otherwise, we kept the paraffin lamps filled in the shelters, and rushed to open them on a warning. During July and August, the Luftwaffe was chiefly concerned with aerodromes and ports. London had occasional raids, and in late August three all-night ones. But not very much happened, and theatres remained open, the actors often doing impromptu 'turns' after the play was over, to keep the audience in the house. Londoners began to think that the horrors of air raids had been exaggerated.

In the meanwhile, at the Post, we played darts and had cups of tea on our nights on duty. Part-time volunteers were expected to go round there on two or three evenings a week, for about three hours, and if, after that, a 'yellow' came through on the telephone from Control, a messenger came and banged on our front doors. Thereupon we turned out and patrolled our respective sectors.

The number of full-time wardens was determined by the population. Thus in a thickly built-up area containing blocks of flats there were more full-timers than in the same acreage of smaller houses. Post 2, on which I lived, was composed of several streets and squares of medium-sized houses, and two main roads of almost slum buildings which were in each case our boundaries. We covered an important stretch of railway line. We had eleven full-time wardens. Most of the residents in the district were not in heavy trades, and there was no shortage of good and conscientious part-timers. In this respect we were the best supplied Post in the borough. There were not, as a

9

rule, so many volunteers in an area where most men were engaged in heavy and monotonous work for long hours. But we had a variety of trades, from railway workers, post-office sorters, lawyers, newspapermen, garage hands, to a few of no very definable profession. I added to the variety by 'representing' the theatre.

We seldom discussed wardens' duties as such. It was not till after the raids had started that I became fully aware of the multitudinous things a warden needed to know, from the names of the residents in each house, and which shelter they used, hydrants, cul-de-sacs, danger points in the area, to the whereabouts of the old and infirm who would need help in getting to shelter, telephone numbers, and addresses of rest centres, etc.

After the fall of France there had been alarm and uneasiness in London; in many cases, real fear, though I never heard anyone suggest that we also should throw in the sponge. But between May and September the belief returned that London would never be attacked. People would ask you if you thought there would be raids, and when you said 'yes,' still clung to the idea that the defences would be strong enough to keep them away. Few wardens had this illusion. Most were sure that serious trouble would begin soon. And they waited, in a mixture of dread, expectation, and impatience, wondering whether the Civil Defence plans would really work, and how they themselves would react.

Two months after I joined the Post, I was notified that a training course was being held. By that time we were getting a great many 'yellows' and a few siren warnings, and though nothing came of them, the lecture was abandoned every time that the 'yellow' was signalled.

We were given several lectures on the smells and effects of the different war gases. We were told of the various standards of shelter protection, authorised by the Government. We were taught three ways of dealing with the small incendiary bomb, and we were told that the blast from high explosive travels, like sound, in all directions, and has an outward and a suction wave. That was all.

There was no lecture on what a warden was supposed to do, either in raids or lulls; there was no lecture on what other CD Services were supposed to do, or how the Control Room worked, how an incident should be controlled, what rules existed in regard to public shelters, or the relationship of the warden and the shelter marshal;

there was no instruction about the various report forms, and not even rudimentary first aid. It may have been better in other boroughs. I don't know. The standard certainly improved.

With the knowledge that Lewisite smelt of geraniums, and BBC of bittersweet (a flower that the average Cockney had never even heard of), that blast would travel in all directions, and armed with a tin hat and a whistle, I, and hundreds of others, faced the blitzes which burst on us on September 7th, 1940. Our only asset was our zeal to help.

IF THE GAS RATTLES SOUND

2

September 1940

SEPTEMBER 7th was one of those beautiful early autumn days which feel like spring, and can make even London streets seem fresh and gay. There was hardly a wisp of cloud in the pale blue sky. At 4.43 p.m. the sirens wailed, and the population trooped to the shelters. The women were frankly fussed and ran, grabbing their children by bits of skirt or jacket; one woman rushed down, her hair a pile of soapsuds straight from the Saturday afternoon shampoo; the children were excited; the men made a point of swaggering in front of their womenfolk, and walked slowly and soberly. But nobody was seriously frightened. There had been repeated 'alerts' and a few actual bombs dropped during the preceding weeks. Something might possibly happen this time, but probably not.

Within a few minutes a large V-shaped formation of planes flew over us, heading to the south-east. The tiny machines glinted in the sunlight and looked more like a flock of geese migrating before the winter than hostile aircraft. Soon they were followed by a smaller formation, each silver speck leaving a gossamer tail curving gracefully behind it. The old soldiers were very knowledgeable and told us they were 'ours.' Later that phrase, 'It's one of ours,' became one of my chief superstitions, so often was it followed by the whistle and crump of bombs.

But that afternoon the danger was still remote from us. It was the East End that was 'getting it.' From where we were we could see the miniature silver planes circling round and round the target area in such perfect formation that they looked like a children's toy model of flying boats or chair-o-planes at a fair. It was almost impossible to imagine that they were doing damage. Occasionally there would be a few puffs of Ack-Ack, but they were too low to interrupt the rhythm of the formations. As one set of planes flew off, another

V-formation would fly in, stretch out into a 'follow-my-leader' line, and circle round as its predecessor had done.

Presently we saw a white cloud rising; it looked like a huge evening cumulus, but it grew steadily, billowing outwards and always upwards. A fire-engine went by up the main road. The cloud grew to such a size that we gasped incredulously; there could not ever in history have been so gigantic a fire. Another fire-engine raced by, then a third, then a fourth, clanging their bells frenziedly as they shot across the traffic lights; our local sub-station turned out, nearly every fire appliance in London was heading east.

As evening drew on, the barrage balloons turned pink in the sunset light; or was it the firelight? They looked pretty enough, but the enormous cloud turned an angrier red, and blackened round the edges. From our vantage-point it was remote and, from a spectacular point of view, beautiful. One had to force oneself to picture the misery and the havoc down below in the most overcrowded area of London; the panic and the horror when suddenly bombs had fallen in the busy, narrow street markets and bazaars, and on the rickety houses.

We were only four miles from this horror, but no one had any conception of what it was like. When the 'all clear' sounded at 6.15 p.m. people left the shelters saying 'About time too,' little realising what lay in store for themselves. We sensed that real air-raids had begun at last, that all the talk about our ground defences being too strong for them was just so much journalese and Blimpery, but we did not yet take the full measure of the coming blitz. I felt, myself, that that was to-day's raid, and that we should probably have another to-morrow, but went off to Soho for dinner that evening. It was not, technically, one of my nights on duty; but it is surprising, on looking back, that one could have made such a nonchalant miscalculation. I had not immediately grasped the principle that an important part of incendiary raids was to provide a beacon for later bombing. I was annoyed when the siren went again before we had even reached the coffee.

When we came out of the restaurant we stopped aghast. The whole sky to the east was blazing red. The afternoon spectacle was completely dwarfed; it seemed as though half of London must be burning, and fifty thousand firemen would not be able to put out a fire of that size. In Shaftesbury Avenue, five miles from the blaze,

Above: Salvaging a few personal belongings after a raid

Below: The massive column of smoke over the docks

it was possible to read the evening paper. Some planes were overhead, but one still had the false confidence of the afternoon that the docks were the target, and that these machines had empty bomb racks. With a whine and a crash a bomb fell somewhere near Charing Cross and the pavement trembled. It was the first time that I had heard a bomb, and in that instant I realised that the whole of London was a target area, and that Piccadilly and King's Cross were as important as the Albert Dock, and any street might get its share. We had to walk most of the way home; it was an unpleasant journey, but one could hardly be missing on the first real raid.

When we got back, I found my senior warden; he was known as 'B.B.' since his name was B. Bartholomew; I did not know his Christian name, in fact I never enquired, as he was too dignified for most of the names beginning with B, and the nickname was a convenient way out of a slightly delicate situation. He and Ruth Morrison, young Jackie and Tommy Brickman, usually known as Bricks, were standing in a cluster in the street; with my arrival we reached the full complement for our sector; all but Bricks were part-timers. We visited the shelters. They had been apprehensive before, now they were distinctly nervous, although few showed real fright.

A warden from the next sector arrived back from his work in the East End. He gave us a graphic account, and insisted on going into each shelter, and telling them of the gigantic fires—'five miles of them'—and the damage, and the casualties, the blood and the horrors, and how he had had to crawl on his belly along the streets. It was hardly a wise thing to do, and at the third telling a large lady with two children told him, with emphasis, where he could go with his belly-crawling.

By 10 p.m. the shelterers were growing exasperated; if it did not stop soon it would be past 'closing time'! By midnight they were frightened. Very few of them had imagined that they would have to sit in a shelter for more than an hour or so; neither for that matter, and more inexcusably, had the authorities. They had not brought rugs or blankets or provisions, some even had no coats, as it had been a warm evening. The wooden benches round the walls were packed, and the remainder had to stand, or sit on bits of newspaper on the concrete floor: the overcrowding was appalling, and the air stank.

B.B. had been in the last war and was very calm and cheerful now, but the rest of us wardens had no idea of distance or direction of these 'objects dropped from the air,' and hurried down the steps or into doorways every time that we heard the whistle of a bomb. However, I found that the bombs terrified me less than did the people in the shelters. It had not before occurred to me that a warden would be expected not only just to poke his head round the door to see if there was anything wrong, but to chat to one and all, and try to cheer them up. In all the nine shelters that came within our province I knew only two people slightly. I was horribly embarrassed, and envied B.B. and Ruth who seemed to know everyone and chatted easily with them all, while I stood awkwardly by the door, smiled stupidly, and could say nothing. One of the good things about the war, however, was the friendliness that the common danger evoked, and comparatively soon I realised that the mere sight of a tin hat gave people a spurious sense of confidence, and that they were really pleased to see one. Whereas before few of us had even known our next-door neighbour, within a week people called good morning to one from their bedroom windows, and we chatted in the grocer's as though we were villagers. Later, I had cause to visit every shelter in the borough, and I doubt if many people have as large and varied a circle of acquaintances as I collected.

By 3 a.m. the raid was heavier than ever and the bombs were much closer—they came down with a tearing sound as well as a whistle; they did not fall, they rushed at enormous velocity, as though dragged down towards the earth by some supernaturally gigantic magnet. Planes began to circle steadily and monotonously overhead, just as we had seen them circling over the East End in the afternoon. It was alarming to feel that this time it was we who were the target: sticks of four, sticks of six, came crashing down, and still the planes circled above, and the houses rocked and trembled. I was alarmed. One hadn't got a chance. For half an hour the bombs pounded down all round us; as one struck another started on its downward journey, and we crouched in the doorways thinking that the next one *must* get us. But we were wrong; neighbouring sectors were hit; ours was let off unscathed.

Three streets away a trench shelter was struck and wrecked, but by a miracle only one man was killed. Vast old Mrs. Magg, who had a reputation for the richest language in the borough, used that shelter: now she was buried up to the neck and, mustering all her talent, 'effed and blinded somethin' 'orrible.' It was a great relief both to her and to the wardens, just as the porter's earthy and obscene grumbling in *Macbeth* is a relief after the tenseness of the murder. She blasphemed, and cursed the wardens for a set of lazy bastards who wouldn't lift a finger to get her out; but two days later she stood all that Post a round of drinks, and remarked, in parenthesis, that she had been a little excited the other night, they were not really such a bad lot.

At dawn the 'all clear' went, and groups of pale and jaded people trailed back to their homes to snatch a cup of tea before leaving for work. They were cold and exhausted and subdued: 'D'you think we'll get another to-night, Miss?' they asked. It was as well that they could not know that they were to get 'another' for fifty-seven nights on end, and after that some raids that were going to make this night's look like child's play. All the rumours of war, and the warnings of aerial bombardment of the last five years, all the bombing of the Spanish towns, the destruction of Warsaw and Rotterdam, had not made them pause to think what it might be like when it came to them, and they were shocked and stunned.

That day London had changed. It was not only the damage, the shattered houses and the glass in the streets, often inches deep. And it was not a melodramatic change; it was more like a drunk man suddenly sobering up when he receives tragic news. At last people realised that there was a serious war on—a war that meant visible death and destruction, not only newspaper articles and recruiting posters and war memorials. And they did not like the realisation.

For troops who have been training and waiting for months, the long-expected attack can often give a sense of relief as well as alarm. But the British public had not had any training, physical or moral, to help it to withstand the nervous strain of being bombed. The ordinary man had not cared deeply about the betrayal of Czechoslovakia at Munich, although he knew that it was shameful, but he had cared less about the Poles. If he troubled to justify the declaration of war at all, it was on technical grounds that if we continued to give way to Hitler there would soon be no allies and no battlegrounds left. The first year of the war with its 'patrol activity' in front of the Maginot Line was commonly accepted as mystifying and ridiculous, and then dismissed as other people's business. Ten days before France collapsed, when I had expressed anxiety in the local pub as to what

ARP teams working in the rubble of former homes

might happen if that country gave in, my remarks were received with indignation and scorn. When the collapse came, the French and the Belgians were just 'dirty traitors.' It was as simple as that. Only one person in twenty genuinely thought that the war was anything to do with him. Indeed, enthusiastic support could hardly be expected when so many people had friends or relations in factories, who were being told to go to the lavatory for an hour, or otherwise waste their time, because there was insufficient work to do.

The newspapers told the country that London could take it. But locally there were sour comments on what journalists knew about it. If London at that stage had been bombed as heavily and continuously as Cologne and Stalingrad, one hesitates to think what might have happened. In the last war there had been the pious cliché that the strain was nearly as great for those safely in the rear as for 'the loved ones at the front.' This time it was true, and the most common saying by men, as well as women, was that this wasn't war, it was murder, they wouldn't stand for it, and so on. The loudest cry, however, was: where were the guns? Where were these defences that had been praised as impassable?

All through Sunday and Monday the East Enders drifted miserably westwards, looking for shelters; most of them had no baggage; they had lost everything; some carried pathetic and clumsy bundles of their remaining belongings; some pushed battered perambulators stacked with salvaged, broken treasures. They had nowhere to rest, nowhere to wash. In the West End attempts were made even to exclude them from some shelters. On a 38 bus in Piccadilly a wretched-looking woman with two children got in and sat down next to me; they still had blast dust in their hair and their tattered clothing; they were utterly miserable, and the lady opposite moved her seat and said, loudly, that people like that should not be allowed on buses. Fortunately, the conductor announced with promptitude that some ladies could take taxis.

In our district, and in others where they could afford it, many who had refused the official evacuation schemes now hurriedly left London. Some went to relatives. They had been unwilling to do so before; wives disliked the idea of playing second fiddle to a sister, or aunt, or cousin, and of living in a house which was not their own home; and this pride as well as a strong tradition of 'wait and see' had kept them back. Others just left for the country with no destina-

Lorryloads of homeless survivors

tion in view. There were queues at the stations and people bought tickets for any place whose name they knew; they had no idea whether there would be any accommodation available, and frequently it turned out that there wasn't. The WVS struggled manfully with hordes of clamouring families, and the railway staffs controlled the crowds admirably. Although there was much tedious waiting and confusion, there was no panic. Clearly, however, a great many of London's population could not leave, and many wives stayed behind to keep alive that strongest tradition of all—the husband's dinner.

Sunday, Monday and Tuesday nights were the same. Bombs pounded down all through the night, many of them unpleasantly close; but none actually in our sector. The nearest was a hundred yards from our boundary. It was a large size in bombs and crashed right through an underground railway tunnel, making a spectacular crater. It just missed an important works, and a row of houses. There was only one casualty. The questions about our defences grew more bitter; men angrily recalled statements in the press to the effect that our AA guns were so powerful and so accurate that enemy planes would never be able to do much more than cross the coast. In Kent one could watch the fighter planes at work, and feel that someone at least was fighting back, but for Londoners there was only a nightmare feeling of impotence; the throbbing Nazi planes could drop their bombs when and where they liked, nobody was doing anything to stop them, and one could only wait for annihilation.

But on Wednesday they brought up the guns at last. Soon after 8.30 p.m. the inevitable droning started, and with an almighty roar the gunners let fly. There was never such an exhilarating uproar; the heavy guns boomed and the light ones cracked; they rattled and split the window-panes. It was a splendid and deafening cacophony. It was said that they fired 20,000 shells that night; it may have been extravagant, and not particularly effective, but it was worth it. It revived the spirits of the Londoners, as a heavy thunderstorm will after a long spell of sultry August weather. (Into the bargain, the death-roll was reduced to a fifth.) The 'fire and crack of sulphurous roaring' continued throughout the night, and made us laugh for joy even at 3 a.m. Some of the shelters were not quite so pleased as we were: they could sleep through a good deal of bombing, but no one could sleep through this hullaballoo, and many of the old ladies were frightened by the sheer noise. But we envied the sweating gunners at their work and I would have given a pound to be allowed one crack myself. During the next few weeks any RA man could be certain of being stood drinks all round the bar.

Four days later came the climax of the air battle. When the evening raid started, 85 enemy planes had been shot down that day. An hour later the BBC interrupted its programme to announce that the number now reported was almost 100; by midnight it was 132. Each time that there was a new announcement B.B. and I went round the shelters with the news, and excitement mounted with the figures. By morning there was the spectacular, incredible total of 185. A 'bag' of that size was worth some bombing.

The heartening effect of the Ack-Ack and the fighter planes was permanent. Once they were assured that some effort was at last being made, that they were not to be abandoned to the bombs without any retaliation being organised, Londoners settled down to their new and strange life with a dogged equanimity, which was an unspectacular form of genuine courage. Many of the habits of a lifetime were rudely changed; sometimes for the better. Wives, for instance, who suffered from snoring husbands, found allies in the new community life. But where they could stick to old habits, they did, even if the idiom had to be changed. I was standing by a surface shelter one night as a couple emerged. The gunfire was getting heavy, and the girl was anxious—'I can't stop now, Tom, really. I must get down the shelter. Mum will be worrying. But I'll meet you to-morrow, same time, same sand-bag.'

3

'First Blood'

My first incident occurred one afternoon in the second week. A soldier, however highly trained, will yet be apprehensive about his own reactions when, for the first time, he actually comes under fire. I had been fairly confident that I could behave reasonably well under gunfire and bombing, and the first seven nights had, more or less, justified my confidence. But what I was very unsure of was what my reactions to casualties would be. I had never seen a dead body, I was even squeamish about handling dead animals, and I was terrified that I might be sick when I saw my first entrails, just as some people cannot stop themselves fainting at the sight of blood. At later incidents one forgot oneself entirely in the job on hand. But on this occasion, because I was unsure of myself, I was acutely self-conscious, and, as a protection, adopted as detached an attitude as I could. I had to watch myself, as well as the objective situation.

It was a grey, damp afternoon in late September, ten days after the start of the air-blitz on London. I was bicycling along a shabby street in a district some miles from my own. The day alerts were so frequent that it was difficult to remember whether the last wailing of the siren had been the alert or the 'all clear.'

It was a street of narrow houses, so decrepit that they might well have crumbled to pieces had they not been held up by occasional large office buildings, and even these were dingy and decayed. Dirty shop windows announced that they were high-class laundries, or would mend your boots while you waited, or would buy cast-off clothing. The whole derelict street and the lanes leading into it were calling for the house-breaker. A little further on, however, in a side turning on the right, the LCC had made a start, and a block of balconied workers' flats had been erected. They were well designed, and the plaster facings and the brickwork were still unsooted by London's grime.

The desolation of the loss of a lifetime's home

Suddenly, before I heard a sound, the shabby, ill-lit, five-storey building ahead of me swelled out like a child's balloon, or like a Walt Disney house having hiccups. I looked at it in astonishment, that bricks and mortar could stretch like rubber. At the point when it must burst, the glass fell out. It did not hurtle, it simply cracked and dropped out, allowing the straining building to deflate and return to normal. Almost instantaneously there was a crash and a double explosion in the street to my right. As the blast of air reached me I left my saddle and sailed through the air, heading for the area railings. The tin hat on my shoulder took the impact, and as I stood up I was mildly surprised to find that I was not hurt in the least. The corner buildings had diverted the full force of blast; indeed, to judge by the number of idiotic thoughts that raced through my head, my progress to the railings might almost have been in 'slow motion.' I had not heard any whistle of the bombs coming down, only the explosion, and now the sound of an aeroplane's engine starting up. I thought, 'So it's true—you don't hear the one that gets, or nearly gets, you.'

For no reason except that one handbook had said so, I blew my whistle. An old lady appeared in her doorway and asked, 'What was all that?' I told her it was a bomb, but she was stone-deaf and I had to abandon bawling for pantomime of a bomb exploding before she would agree to go into a surface shelter. After putting a dressing on some small cuts on a man's face, I turned back towards the site of the damage. I did not know the locality, but, again, the handbook said that when an alert sounded, a warden away from his home area should report to the nearest Post. The damage was thirty yards away, but the corner building, which had diverted some of the blast from me, was still standing.

At four in the afternoon there would certainly be casualties. Now I would know whether I was going to be of any use as a warden or not, and I wanted to postpone the knowledge. I dared not run. I had to go warily, as if I were crossing a minefield with only a rough sketch of the position of the mines—only the danger-spots were in myself. I was not let down lightly. In the middle of the street lay the remains of a baby. It had been blown clean through the window, and had burst on striking the roadway. To my intense relief, pitiful and horrible as it was, I was not nauseated, and found a torn piece of curtain in which to wrap it. Two HE bombs had fallen on the new flats, and a third on an equally new garage opposite. In all this grimy derelict area, they had struck the only decent habitations.

The CD services arrived quickly. There was a large number of 'white hats,' but as far as one could see no one person took charge, and there were no blue incident flags. I offered my services, and was thanked but given nothing to do, so busied myself finding blankets to cover the five or six mutilated bodies in the street. A small boy, aged about 13, had one leg torn off and was still conscious, though he gave no sign of any pain. In the garage a man was pinned under a capsized Thorneycroft lorry, and most of the side wall and roof were piled on top of that. The Heavy Rescue Squad brought ropes, and heaved and tugged at the immense lorry. They got the man out, unconscious, but alive. He looked like a terra-cotta statue, his face, his teeth, his hair, were all a uniform brick colour.

Eleven had been killed but a larger number were badly injured— an old man staggered down supported by two girls holding a towel to his face; as we laid him on a stretcher the towel dropped, and his face was shockingly cut away by glass. It was astonishing that he had been able to walk down stairs. Three more stretcher cars and two ambulances arrived, but they had to park some distance away because of the débris. If they had been directed to approach from the western side they could have driven much closer. The wardens began to check up the flats. As I did not know the residents, or how many of them there ought to be, I could not help, and stayed below.

But by now the news had travelled, and women back from shopping, girls, and a few men from local factories, came running and scrambling over the débris in the street. 'Where is Julie?' 'Is my Mum· all right?' I was besieged, but I could not help them. They shouted the names of their relatives and scanned the faces of the dusty, dishevelled survivors. Those who found that they had lost a relation seemed numbed by the shock and were quiet, whereas a woman who found her family intact promptly had hysterics. The sudden relief from an awful fear was more unnerving at the moment than the confirmation of the fear.

A little later I left: there was nothing apparently that I could do, little enough that I had done. Any bystander could have been as helpful as I had been, and I felt discouraged and depressed. My bicycle was bent, but since the wheels would still go round, I clanked and wobbled on it back to my own Post.

Overleaf: Stunned survivors often had to be led firmly from their wrecked homes

Tommy Brickman was there, and greeted me with 'Blimey, your face!' I explained how it had got so dirty, and noticed, to my amusement, that he was obviously chagrined that it had been I, and not himself, who had 'had the fun.' Tommy was an energetic and conscientious warden, but both imaginative and loquacious. His existence was a continous conversation piece with no back answers allowed. At the same time, he was quite incapable of seeing only six German planes, or being missed by only a 50-kg. bomb, or of extinguishing only a dozen incendiaries; it had always to be 60 planes, a 1,000-kg. bomb, or hundreds of incendiaries at least. If Tommy went away for a day or so to another town, we knew that that town would have 'the biggest blitz ever.' If he travelled by train, that train was machine-gunned. It was a habit that irritated the more serious-minded members of the Post, though I could not myself see that it mattered whether Tommy's graphic and hair-raising accounts were in fact true or not. I think he found me a pleasant audience, as I always egged him on by asking innocent questions. However, this time it was *my* story.

Tommy made me some tea, but before we had time to drink it, the evening siren went, and I left for my sector post. It was another all-night session and the 'all clear' did not sound until 6.15 a.m. We were supposed to wait, however, until we received the 'white' on the telephone, and I waited irritably for half an hour, angry with Control for being so inconsiderate of us after a twelve-hour raid. But when the man who lived in the flat above our post came down, he pointed out that Jim Mackin, the Post Warden, had come round at midnight to tell me that the phone was out of order.

To my alarm, I found that I could not remember that, or anything else after reporting for duty at 6.30 p.m. I replied, 'Oh yes, of course,' but as I walked home I tried to reconstruct the evening. I remembered the incident in the afternoon, but the twelve hours after that were a complete blank; I could not even remember whether I had gone home for supper. I counted the plates in the kitchen, but that did not tell me anything, and I was really frightened as I waited for someone in the house to get up. For all I knew I might have made an awful fool of myself. Apparently, I had behaved quite normally, made my usual tour of the shelters, had supper, and helped someone to change the wheel of his car, but I still could not remember any of it. I had one hazy picture of a white hat in a doorway, which must have been Jim Mackin, but that was all. If I was to have that sort of reaction after every incident, it was going to be inconvenient.

I had learnt several things from that first incident. I had been fairly confident, though certainly not sure, that I could control my nerves, but now I also knew that I was not liable to nausea—an affliction which is much less controllable. I had learnt that a warden can be of very little use off his own area, and in fact is not particularly welcome—seldom, after that, did I visit any incident that was not 'ours,' unless I was sent there officially. Thirdly, I learnt that there was insufficient co-ordination between the separate CD Services: no one person had been in charge, and there had been no obvious reporting post. In theory, the warden reported an incident from his Post telephone, the Heavy Rescue Service did the digging and releasing, the Stretcher Party* put the victim on a stretcher, the Ambulance loaded and conveyed that stretcher to a hospital. At practice exercises this arrangement worked excellently, but in an actual raid, when it was generally pitch dark, when there were incidents in all directions, when the telephones often broke down, there were frequently a waste of both personnel and time.

Wardens came under the jurisdiction of the Local Authority, and their treatment and conditions varied in each borough. The Heavy Rescue came under the LCC, the Stretcher Party and First Aid Posts under the Local Authority, but the Ambulances, again under the LCC, and the police and the Fire Brigade had their own organisation. There were jealousies arising from the fact that some service was much better looked after than another, members of one service did not know the members of another, and there could certainly have been more co-operation at incidents. Sometimes Heavy Rescue men would snub wardens who tried to help them, at others a warden would say that such and such a job was not his province; I met one Stretcher Party crew who even refused to go into a lightly-damaged building until the Heavy Rescue arrived.

This was rare, but often a bomb would fall on the boundary between one borough and another, and there would be almost acrimonious argument as to which should claim it, and therefore delay. There were official taboos as well: wardens, for instance, were not allowed to plug broken and burning gas-pipes; we had to leave them to the Gas Company squads, who were always overworked;

*The Light Rescue Service later replaced the Stretcher Parties.

yet it is an easy thing to do, and when the blitzes were over a few of us were instructed in the matter. When the warden in charge and the Rescue Leader were sensible there was seldom trouble, but not infrequently at incidents men and women who were genuinely eager to help stood idle because they dared not tread on another's ground.

Finally, I learnt that the training which a warden received was, to say the least, inadequate. No amount of training can teach you everything, but there should be sufficient to assure you that you know what you ought to do in any emergency. An incident hardly ever goes according to the book; but if you have a thorough knowledge of what you are supposed to do, you are very much quicker at thinking of something else that you *can* do. My own case is typical of many. I was extremely anxious to be as helpful as possible, but I had hardly any idea of what, officially, I was supposed to do.

The first fortnight of the blitz was very exhausting. Every night, and all night, there were raids. On the evening of the 16th the 'red' came up at 8.5 p.m., and the final 'white' at 9.15 the next morning. That made thirteen hours, broken by three short 'all clears,' one lasting half an hour, the others ten minutes each. Every day we had two, three, or four raids, of one or two hours' duration. At the end of the fortnight I added it all up, and found that I had done 78 hours of raid duty in the first week and 102 in the second. Clearly, this was over-zealousness on my part; but I had volunteered for just such an emergency, and I could not at first bring myself to ignore an alert. I was so determined to avoid the usual accusation against voluntary helpers—that they do not turn up—that I overdid it. So did most of the others. One morning about 4 a.m. I went back to the Post to report that I was going home. The 'all clear' had gone at 3 a.m., and for an hour it had been quiet. I clanked down the stairs to the basement room. Five of them were lying sprawled on the floor on their coats, dead to the world. The other two were sitting in upright chairs by the telephone, but their heads were sunk on their chests, and only the table prevented them from falling. Despite the noise I had caused, no one stirred. They might have been dead, but for the sighing of their breathing.

We organised it better after the first two weeks, and although we were often exhausted after a heavy night, I, at least, never suffered from the numb, almost paralysing tiredness of the beginning. We

A small part of the effect of a major raid

began to ignore the daytime raids unless something dropped locally, leaving them to the full-timers on the day shift. In any case, most Londoners ignored the daylight attacks, despite the fact that casualties per bomb were relatively heavier. Certainly, mutilations were more severe, and their horrible details more plain to see. But not only were men and women less tired, they felt braver in the daylight. A simple and primitive fear of the dark added to the long-drawn-out strain of the night raids.

On our sector we soon developed a routine; we were the furthest sector from the Post, and as B.B. had a telephone and I had a bicycle, his front room was soon converted into a sort of sub-post. In the intervals between visiting the shelters, or patrolling the streets, we gathered there, if the bombing was not local, and played an elementary game of cards. It was my fault that it was an elementary kind of game, as I do not play cards; in fact, the only thing I like about them is the pictures. Despite this pastime, 3 a.m. to 5 a.m. was a deadly period. One had always smoked too much, and felt jaded and stale. But day after day, the early September mornings were beautiful, with a light frost and a clear pale sky, against which the balloons glowed pink and silver in the sunrise, and planes which had been an ominous threat in the darkness were now sparkling dots, weaving and interweaving their long white scarves in intricate patterns overhead.

Raids had their lighter side.

At half-past one in the morning a message came through on the phone from Control. B.B. took it, said, 'Oh, . . . oh yes, thank you. We'll see to it. Thank you,' very politely, as he put down the receiver, and turned to me to explain. 'They say that there is an enemy object over the main road. The wind, they say is north-easterly, and it is floating in our direction. But as the message has been relayed twice already, it can hardly be going to land here now, and I don't quite see what we are supposed to do about it.' Anyway, we could not see it, so we did nothing.

At half-past two there was another message from Control. This time it was said that a German parachutist had landed in Lloyd Square, where I lived, and we were to search for him. The police turned out with revolvers and made a ring round the area; everyone seemed to be taking it very seriously, and B.B. and I searched back-gardens. I immediately fell off a wall and hurt myself, and began to think the proceedings were ridiculous. Even provided that there had really been a parachutist, if he were an airman, he would probably have broken at least one leg on a chimney-pot, and in any case would not fight; and if he were a genuine parachutist, a Fifth Columnist, he would have come down dressed as a warden and we should have directed him very politely to the next borough. We searched some more backyards. Three large bombs screamed over us very low and landed on the railway line just across our boundary. The draught of their passage rocked the porch we were in. We decided that looking for parachutists was a wholly ridiculous proceeding—and abandoned it.

There was a great deal of 'jitteriness' about parachutists—in London it was rather ludicrous. Since Essex and Surrey offered far greater amenities for landing, and were reasonably handy, it was not likely that anyone would risk all the chimney-pots and roof-tops of London—let alone the trolley-bus wires. But once, when an attachment broke loose from a local balloon site, and two of the men traced it to a roof-top some distance away, they were stopped by police and Home Guards, who told them that there were twelve German parachutists with automatic rifles on the roof, and they were compelled to telephone their Squadron Headquarters before they were allowed to retrieve their property.

Our first incendiaries gave us a lively night, but as they only descended in dozens, not in thousands, we managed them very easily. The public, and most wardens, persisted in calling these showers Molotov Breadbaskets, in spite of articles and diagrams in the press, which showed that the whole point of the Breadbasket was a considerable poundage of high explosive contained in the same case as a number of small incendiaries. The ones we received in this country were scattered from simple tin containers, and even when the second development took place and some explosive was inserted in each small bomb, it was only a matter of a couple of ounces. Their dangerous quality lay in their numbers.

We were standing in the doorway of our sector post when our first shower descended with a rattle and clatter. An HE comes down with purpose and direction, but incendiaries sound more like an accident with a tray full of tin cans, and it is difficult to believe that they can be responsible for such a holocaust as they created in the City later. Most of them fell in the road, and we ran about with zest, dumping sandbags on them. Bricks managed to find a shower of his own, which he said were explosive ones, but no one believed him. Mine certainly were not.

One or two fell in houses and needed stirrup pumps, and I made the great mistake of getting landed with the pumping. One has to learn these things. The first bucketful is easy, the second begins to be irritating, by the third one becomes breathless, by the fourth exasperated, and one wishes the plunger had more resistance so that one could work it more slowly, instead of jigging up and down at an exhausting speed. Jackie had had one all to himself: it had fallen on to a Miss Heywood's bed, on the top floor of No. 8, and he had dumped two buckets of earth and three of water on to it, and said it was now 'all OK.'

We had a wash and were sitting down for a smoke, rather pleased with ourselves, when there was another clatter, and out we dashed again. This time more of them struck houses, and one got a good hold on an empty cottage. As it was locked and shuttered, the smoke was almost solid by the time we managed to break in; but I was not going to get caught a second time, and commandeered the nozzle. A room with wooden walls at the far side was blazing merrily, the flames augmented by broken gas-pipes, but when once I reached the room itself the air was distinctly clearer, so that when someone crawled along to relieve me I truthfully said that I preferred the atmosphere where I was. It was like a well-staged demonstration exercise, and very enjoyable, only marred at the end by young Jackie emptying the hose-pipe all down me.

Throughout the night, as soon as we had dealt with one shower, another would come down, but we only had to call the Fire Brigade once. A bomb had lodged in the thickness of the wall in a top storey, and the children's choppers with which we were issued were not strong enough to tackle it—the blades were only cast-metal and snapped at a tap. As I went down the stairs to send a report the old lady of the house clutched me, '*Don't* send for the Fire Brigade, miss; oh don't, miss, please.' She preferred the top storey to burn out rather than have all her furniture swamped. But there was a danger of its spreading to the next house, the report had to be sent, and soon her chairs and carpets were floating in gallons of water. Most firemen were as considerate as possible in poor people's homes, but, generally, there was no option.

While the firemen worked at that one, Jackie and I took another look at Miss Heywood's bed. Under the pile of earth, all the bedding and the mattress were smouldering, and the iron frame was red hot. It took us a long time to cut it all up with my penknife, cart the flock and blankets downstairs in a galvanised bath, and spread it out in the street. It looked a sorry sight, and we decided that we should be wiser not to be there when Miss Heywood came home in the morning.

By 4 a.m. the extinguishing of incendiaries was no longer enjoyable; one's legs and arms ached from running up and down stairs with buckets. So when B.B. pointed out the light of a fire showing through a window at 4.30 a.m., I sighed.

'That's across the road, it's the next borough,' he said.

'Yes,' I said, and we stood in the middle of the street gazing pensively at the glowing window.

'*Perhaps* we ought to go.'

'It isn't our ground.'

'Nobody seems to be about.'

'They're a lazy lot.'

'Oh, perhaps we had better just go and see whether it is a bad one.'

It was a dark and dirty little house, one of a dingy row below the street level. The bedding and the upholstered furniture were burning, and the woodwork was blazing quite brightly. The smell was foul. The flames subsided quickly, and as we wearily tossed the mattress and quilts out of the window we continued to grumble at the wardens of this borough—'Lazy lot of loafers, they're probably having a nice cup of tea, while we do their work!'

A week later the main Post was just missed by an oil bomb, which the wardens managed to smother without having to call in the NFS, and on our sector we had more small incendiaries. About midnight I heard Bricks shouting and blowing his whistle. I had not heard any clatter, but supposed it was more fires. I picked up a stirrup pump and a bucket of water, and, cursing and weary, lumbered off at a trot in his direction, wishing that someone would invent a bucket that did not slop all down your legs. When I got there, there was great excitement. 'Look,' said Bricks, 'up there. Did you see it?' In case we did not know he told us what it was. One should have been alarmed, but I was furious. Why, I demanded, did he have to blow his——whistle and make me cart all this blasted muck about? Bricks said he was sorry, he had thought that we would like to see; but I was very unreasonable. At that moment someone shouted that there was another one coming down.

They landed across the main road. Bricks shouted, 'Everybody lie down,' and as we did so there was a huge flash and explosion: actually they were almost instantaneous since it was so close, but I remember having time to calculate, as I lay on the pavement and gripped the railing, whether I did not expose more of my person in a prone than an upright position. Then came the bricks and the dust and the glass, but none of us was hurt, and I returned to the argument about whistle-blowing. Whistles, I said, should be kept for fires, otherwise one simply increased the number of people in danger, since volunteers always emerged from the shelters to help with incendiaries. Before, however, I had time to develop my thesis fully, a third came down and we all lay flat on our faces again. Nothing happened. It had struck a refrigerator factory, but still nothing happened; we stood up. It must be UX. To everyone's annoyance I returned again to my argument. It seems now incredible that one could have been so casual about them, but this was our first experience of the kind. I happened to be right, but it was scarcely the most suitable moment for discussion. A week later another came down our way and caused colossal damage—the most extensive I had yet seen.

In many of the books about the First World War the authors asserted that they found being bombed was a far greater strain than being shelled. I have never been shelled—except once, by accident, on a walking holiday—so am incapable of comparing the two; but, unpleasant as it was, I found bombing at least slightly less horrifying than my imagination had pictured it. Even when nothing hit your particular square half-mile, it was certainly a considerable nervous strain hearing an almost continuous whistle or scream of bombs on all sides, particularly when it went on night after night for months. The whistle by itself made your stomach turn over. But when an ordinary HE was really coming your way, there was only time to lie down. There was no alternative, and almost no suspense—only a flashing second of hope. It cannot be nearly so nerve-racking as setting out on a long-distance bombing raid over defended country. Yet we met several airmen who seemed to like being bombed even less than we did. Strangely, perhaps it was just a question of habit.

There was a widely held belief in the early days that a place, or house, once bombed, would be immune from further visitations. It may have been based on a misapplication of the theory of inoculation, or possibly on an inverted version of the saying, 'Once bitten, twice shy'; perhaps it was only due to optimism. But, as a result, when a small 50-kg. landed on the kerb outside my front door, blew in all the doors and windows on that side of the square, but caused no casualties at all, all the residents were very pleased. All, except Mrs. Gervase. She was, to judge by the innumerable photographs covering the walls of her front parlour, the widow of an Edwardian officer in the Indian Army, and the next morning she was making an unwarrantable fuss about the really negligible damage, till one of the men working in the crater had the resourcefulness to tell her that it had been a 1,000-kg. Whereupon she went off much cheered, to write to her nieces and nephews that she had had the biggest bomb yet in her square!

My misgivings on this theory of immunity, however, were rudely confirmed three weeks later, when another 'fifty' landed eight yards further away, but again exactly opposite my front door. This time it was the gardener who was distressed; his tulip bed had been ruined. I doubt if any other bomb damage caused him quite such bitter heartbreak. In April we had a third and larger HE in the square. But we were only a minor instance of innumerable such cases in all parts of London; one of the most disastrous being a Fire Brigade station, which on three separate occasions suffered 1,000-kg. bombs within yards of each other. The reverse of the popular fancy seemed to contain more truth.

4

October–November

RAIDING was not so heavy during the last weeks of October, but the face of London was changing. It was impossible to make a direct journey; at about every third street one was confronted with a yellow 'Diversion' notice. Unexploded bombs—'UXB's'—were everywhere. At first the papers had referred to these 'time-bombs,' as they were then called, as a particularly devilish German invention, despite the fact that since they provided time to evacuate residents in the neighbourhood, they were in reality more humane than the reverse. A few people were exceptionally stupid about them, and would wheedle their way back past the police at the barrier on the excuse of a pet or indispensable treasure left behind, in order, presumably, to boast that they had stayed all night over a UXB. They caused considerable transport difficulties, which was the intention, but the police were extremely quick at putting up the notices; they were almost always in position within an hour of dawn, and buses threaded their unwieldy bulk down narrow side streets that were only meant to take a coster's barrow, and blundered through secluded squares which had never been violated by a public vehicle before.

Buses from Glasgow, Birmingham, Leeds, and sea-side resorts, began to appear; grey buses, chocolate buses, maroon buses; they looked oddly out of place, and one had an absurd feeling of gratitude to the people of those cities for helping us out, although one knew that they were either owned by the same company, or that a normal business transaction had taken place.

London grew shabbier. Even the West End began to look derelict. Gay and flashy Shaftesbury Avenue was very largely boarded up. Everywhere the dust of 'incidents' lay thickly on top of the usual London grime. Windows were gaping black holes, and gave the houses a mournful and blind appearance. By degrees these wounds

Above: The inevitable queue for food in short supply
Below: 'Buses from Glasgow, Birmingham, Leeds and sea-side resorts began to appear'

were dressed with canvas by the first-aid repairers, but they still looked like lacerated creatures patched up with sticking plaster. In the poor quarters of London many people had to live by gaslight (if the gas was still working), or in the dark; their homes were sealed and only draughts, rather than air, reached them. Many never took off their clothes. At Christmas, when raids were lighter, the old lady in the newspaper shop asked me if I thought it was now safe for her to undress; she hadn't, she said, had her clothes off since September, and she was *so* tired. Many who used the tubes and other shelters went there straight from their factories, in their working clothes. In the morning they left their bedding in the cloakroom, or got 'mum' to take it home, and went back to their work. Only once a week could they get a proper wash.

Hundreds of bombed-out cats slunk through the débris, hunting the mice and rats, and ransacking the garbage tins. Cats that had been sleek, well-fed pets, grew as thin as their scavenging mangy brothers that are such a notorious feature of the churches and the squares in Rome. Some had simply been turned loose when the family evacuated. One little old lady whom I knew, collected sixteen of these 'poor pussies' in her basement flat; she would have collected even more if the 'ground floor' had not protested. The police and the RSPCA did their best, but the animals quickly grew wild and crafty.

Some families tried to take their dogs with them into shelters, and were heartbroken when we had to insist on turning them out. For childless couples and single people, their dog was often their child. But it could not be allowed. Apart from hygienic reasons, an animal's reactions to a nearby bomb burst are unpredictable, and it was not safe. Every evening for a week, when the siren sounded, a large brown dog rushed wildly through our square and down the hill, its tail between its legs, howling as it went. We said that it must be making for a West End deep shelter. But on the seventh night it did not appear: either the police or a bomb splinter must have caught it. Fortunately, the majority of dogs had been evacuated or destroyed, but sometimes one would howl for hours in an empty house, thereby adding considerably to our nervous discomfort.

Human casualties from bombing were quieter than I, personally, had expected. Only twice did I hear really terrifying screaming, apart from hysteria: one night a signalman had his legs blown off, and while he was still conscious his box burst into flames; it was utterly impossible for anyone to reach him, and it seemed an age before his ghastly, paralysing screams subsided. Usually, however, casualties, even those who were badly hurt or trapped, were too stunned to make much noise. Animals, on the other hand, made a dreadful clamour. One of the most unnerving nights of the first three months was when a cattle market was hit, and the beasts bellowed and shrieked for three hours: a locomotive had been overturned at the same time and its steam-whistle released. The high-pitched monotonous note, coupled with the dismal roaring of the bullocks, was maddening. It was all a mile from our boundary and there was nothing that we could do to help, but I noticed that we all grew rather bad-tempered and nervous.

Animals' panic is almost as infectious as that of human beings. London's stablemen deserve far more credit than they have ever received. Few people realise how many horses are kept in London. On the night of the City fire, a large firm of carters caught alight along with all the surrounding streets, and the two stablemen, with one or two volunteers, led 200 horses to safety. Some London stables have since adopted the country custom of keeping a goat among their horses—the goat can be led out, and the horses will follow it.

It was in October, five days after Mr. Chamberlain had resigned from the Government, that Mr. Churchill surveyed the view from Primrose Hill, and announced cheerfully that at the current rate of bombing it would take ten years to knock half of London flat. It was a somewhat risky remark to make, as it might easily have been regarded as callous and Olympian from one who, naturally, was provided with more adequate shelter than the majority. But, in fact, they were exactly the right words for the moment. Old ladies, of course, took the statement at its face value, and immediately thought that they were much safer. But even those who realised that such statistics made no difference at all to their personal chance, if they lived in a 'target area,' as we did, were still cheered and amused—'Fancy the 'ole man thinking up that one!' London's sense of humour was reasserting itself, and various quips and pleasantries appeared on the boards that filled in shop windows. Public-houses displayed notices saying: 'With the manager's compliments. This house will remain open at all licensed hours, except in the event of a direct hit.'

In the last week of September 133 planes had been shot down in one day. An official announcement on October 18th declared that a large-scale invasion attempt had been smashed. A week later Mussolini announced that he had formed a special corps of airmen to have its share in bombing London. Everyone laughed, despite the fact that Italian bombs have the same filling as German ones. Three days after that, the Greeks refused the Italian ultimatum and we had a fighting ally. At least something was happening; even if there were not real grounds for our greater optimism. The *Schwarze Korps* explained our attitude by saying that England 'approaches death with sensual pleasure, smacks its lips over every aspect of the conflict.'

In our Post area we were not plunged suddenly into a full-scale blitz as the East End had been. We graduated through incendiaries, two or three oil bombs, two or three small HE's, on our territory, and two truly devastating explosions just on the other side of our boundary road. We began to think that our square mile held a lucky charm. True, most of our streets were residential, but we bordered on two or three important, and therefore legitimate, targets, and no bombing can be expected to be accurate within the width of a road. The rest of the borough was getting burnt and blasted very effectively, but when oil bombs fell on us they landed in, or almost in, the open, and our HE's landed on empty houses or in the streets. (They still sounded alarming enough on the way down, but no one was killed.) Just across the boundary road, in both directions, half a street would be shattered at a blow, and casualties would be numerous. But our luck held. It held until the last two months of the blitz in 1941. Then we were heavily disillusioned.

It may sound callous not to go and help at an incident only a few hundred yards away. But with such widespread bombing as London was getting, it was not wise. Nor was it official policy. If you went off to help your neighbour, you were as likely as not to have something dropped in your own area in your absence. Occasionally, of course, it was necessary. Bricks, however, invariably insisted on dashing off to anything within earshot. On one occasion, a pub on the corner of a side street not far away was hit, and smashed except for the bar. The publican was extremely cheerful and issued an invitation to one and all: 'Come on, gentlemen—drinks on the 'ouse. There ain't no b—— 'ouse, so drinks on it. 'Elp yourselves, gentlemen.' Bricks helped himself to a pint pot of what he thought, in the dark,

44

was brown ale. But it turned out to be port; and a pint tankard of port was too much even for Bricks. As many pubs were hit as churches, and a number of publicans grew nervous and superstitious; but since almost every street in London contains at least one of these buildings, it was natural and inevitable.

On another occasion an oil bomb landed on some stables nearby. Someone said that there were horses there, and two of us went across to see if we could help. I was highly doubtful of my ability to cope with stampeding and screaming horses, but when we arrived we found, to my relief, that the mews only sheltered cars. We pushed a number of these into the street out of reach of the flames, and came back again. The other end of the borough was getting it much more heavily than we were, and a quarter of a mile away there was a shocking disaster when an HE hit a large building which contained a reinforced basement shelter. The whole structure collapsed, and a large water tank and a main burst. One hundred and thirty people, including many children, were crushed or drowned. The entire family of one of our Rescue Service men was buried there. For days on end he watched the digging, although there was no hope at all. They tried to persuade him to go away, but he only shook his head. His wife had wanted to stay at home that night, and he had himself insisted that she and the children go to the shelter.

In November we hoped that the fogs would bring a respite, but although the raids were not heavy, except on the 14th and 15th, the planes were nearly always there, and the bad weather only made things more unpleasant for us.

One Saturday night when it had been quiet for an hour or more, the local parson and the fire-boys had joined us at the sector Post and we were having our simple game of cards. Jackie's eyes were gleaming from the triumph of winning the fabulous sum of $2\frac{1}{2}$d., when we were interrupted by the rushing, tearing sound of a bomb. Someone said, 'Here's ours,' and we all ducked. I wanted to get outside, as I did not think that two wardens, two messengers and a parson all at one blow, and all mixed up with a lot of playing-cards, would create at all a good impression. But there wasn't time, the whole house seemed to move six inches one way and six inches back again.

All the same it was not 'ours,' and we split into parties and went to look for it. B.B. and I reached the main road and found a quantity of glass, and a tangle of trolley-bus posts and wires. I was nervous of these. In theory, if the wires break the supply is bound to be broken. But I did not feel like taking chances with even theoretical electrocution, and I don't think B.B. did either. We knocked at the corner house, which had lost its doors and windows. The owner said he was quite all right, and he thought that the bomb must have been the other side of the road, which would make it the next borough. It was pitch dark and quite impossible to see another person three feet away. We decided to make a detour round the back of the block to avoid the wires. Just as we had made up our minds that it was not on our area, and B.B. was saying that he would go to tell the shelterers that it was 'miles away,' we turned a corner, and there it was. We had been very slow; we must have taken more than five minutes to find a bomb that had dropped less than a hundred yards away. Fortunately, one of the others had been a little quicker.

A row of early nineteenth-century houses in the main road had been hit. They were largely inhabited by Italians, and though shabby and almost of slum standard, each had had a flourishing grape vine climbing up its face, framing the grimy rickety doors, and curling gracefully round the paintless window-frames. Later we found that five had been completely demolished.

But that night there was no moon; there were not even any stars visible, and it was utterly black. Since the houses were old they had crumbled piecemeal; there were no immovable blocks of concrete or heavy girders, and we got eleven people out with such expedition that there was no need to call the Heavy Rescue. The darkness was the greatest obstacle, as we only had our warden's torches; and even then some adolescent members of the Home Guard persisted in bellowing 'Put that light out' every few minutes. The belief was still common that enemy planes, 10,000 feet up, could see the light of a shielded and frosted bicycle lamp, and drop a bomb directly on it. The road was the boundary of the borough, and we had a somewhat heated dispute with the wardens of the other side as to whose incident it was. As a result they set up their incident-reporting post on the opposite side of the road to ours, which was confusing for the stretcher cars and ambulances when they drove up, and therefore wasted time.

Seeing that the houses were completely demolished, it was a miracle that the human damage was not greater. No one had been killed. One woman was hysterical. Screaming and sobbing, she told

October 12th, 1940: the morning after a 'routine' air raid

us that she had had a quarrel with her husband that evening and had locked the bedroom door against him. Only a few moments after he had banged on the door demanding to be let in, with no success, the bomb had struck, and she was now convinced that it was the judgment of God on her for her wickedness. Her husband was extricated ten minutes later. He had only his shirt on, was covered with blast dirt, and at least one leg was broken. She rushed up to him as he was being supported by two of the wardens, but when she saw the state in which he was, she burst out again: 'Oh Bill, Bill! Where's your trousers? Oh Bill, you never ought.' Poor 'Bill' was too close to unconsciousness and too full of dust to bother about her, his trousers, or the encouraging remarks of a small knot of neighbours who had come out of the shelter nearby, some with water and blankets, others merely as sightseers.

In the normal way they would never leave the shelter from warning to all clear, but the predicament of Bill and the others made them oblivious of planes still flying over us, and they clustered round as though it were a peace-time street accident. When I tried to keep a space clear, I was roundly told off for an interfering hussy.

We had a list of the residents and found that two families were missing. A woman gave us the information that one of the families sometimes went to a shelter about a quarter of a mile away. To atone for my slowness in finding the incident I volunteered to try and find them. Still very nervous of being electrocuted, I climbed over the wires, scrambled round and over the débris, and promptly fell into the crater of another bomb which until then we did not know existed. Fortunately it was dry, though half an hour later it started to fill with water, and when Jackie fell into it he was soaked to the armpits.

I was apprehensive of the reception I should get in the shelter; the family that I wanted, and the majority of the users of that shelter, were Italian, and I feared an outburst of hysterical wailing. It was a large shelter holding three or four hundred, and labyrinthine in its construction. All the occupants were asleep, lying on the concrete floor wrapped in blankets and newspaper. I woke two of them and asked for Mrs. Barbirelli. They told me that she was probably in one of the end bays, and went to sleep again. I was angry at their unhelpfulness, but they had to go to work early, and it was difficult to get anything like sufficient sleep those days.

However, a little lame man got up, and, stepping over all the sleeping bundles of humanity, led me to Mrs. Barbirelli. She took the news remarkably well, and only asked, pathetically, 'Is there *anything* left?' Although she had lived in that house for fifteen years she did not know either of the adjoining streets by name, and still less had she any idea of north or south, and since I could not make out which of the various piles of rubble had been hers, I had to give an evasive reply. But she told me that the other missing family usually went all the way to Selfridge's shelter, and had certainly left the house that evening. When I got back the Post Warden was holding a post-mortem on the incident, and I had missed being ticked off for being slow in its discovery. The roll-call was now complete, with the exception of a police inspector who had been buried by the collapse of a wall during the rescue operations. And presently Wally Marshall and another of our wardens came in and said they had got him out.

The incident had been managed more or less creditably, but the same cannot be said of the relief services the next day. Our nearest Rest Centre was a good distance away. There was one fairly close in the adjoining borough, but the people on our side of the street were not eligible for that. It was pouring with rain. The distribution of money, clothes, and cups of tea, each took place in different centres, and one family, two of them only in carpet slippers, had to go to five different addresses.

Another family was given a billet which was lousy. They objected to taking it; but when they went to the Town Hall they were told that they had refused the accommodation offered, and could not, therefore, have any other. The horror of bugs and lice is by no means confined to the upper classes, and it is impertinent of officials to assume, as they do, that anyone who is poorly dressed has no objection to these pests, and no right to any objection. For fourteen days that family lived in the shelter; there was only the door for ventilation and the rain dripped through the roof to such an extent that they had to fix up a borrowed umbrella over their bunks.

There were empty houses and flats belonging to the same estate within 300 yards, and they could have been requisitioned. They were more expensive and the estate agent refused to let them, even temporarily, to people of lower class. Old Mrs. Savery applied for one. She had lived in her house for twenty-three years, and now it was a pile of dust, together with all her furniture and personal treasures. She was refused, and the agent asked her to return her front-door key. Usually she was a mild-tempered woman, but that angered her. 'Key!' she yelled, 'key! When I ain't got no bleedin' front door.'

There were a great many other grievances current at the time. The homeless, locally, were not yet in overwhelming numbers, yet the relief organisation was inadequate. There was no General Information Bureau, and no branch of the Citizens' Advice Bureau, and yet when some of the residents formed a People's Advice Bureau, with the aim of giving information about claims for damage, etc., the Town Hall asserted that this was run by the Communist Party and should be boycotted. No doubt there were Communists on the committee, and, if so, it was surely to their credit. Even in the middle of the miseries of the blitz, party politics and prejudices could not be forgotten, and 'that,' as our Post Warden, Mackin, tartly said, is why France fell.'

But ours was by no means the only borough which did not provide adequate relief organisation; some were far worse. A friend of mine volunteered to help in a dockside area the day after it had been heavily hit. More than a thousand people, bandaged or in need of bandaging, were collected in the Town Hall, and all that the local officials produced as relief fund for this number was £30. Thirty pounds among a thousand people, an inadequate supply of tea handed out as a charity, and no food!

Above : The ARP post open for business in the street
Below : Relief centre in the East End of London

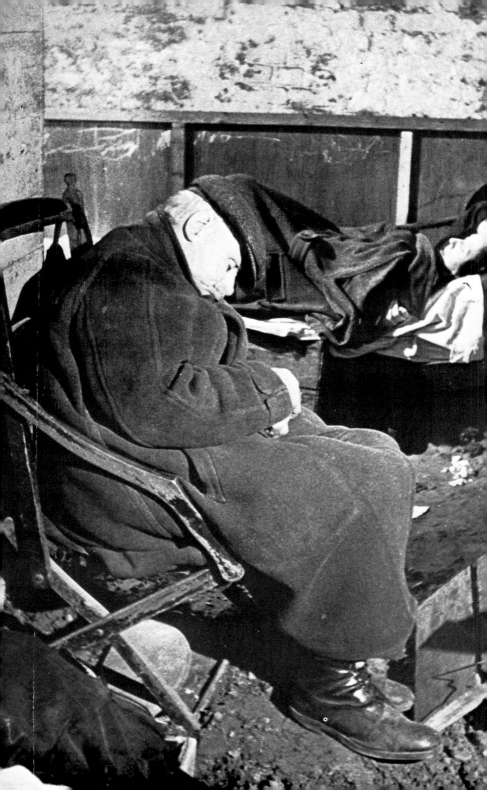

5

Shelters

IT is now generally admitted that during September 1940 the shelter conditions were appalling. In many boroughs there were only flimsy surface shelters, with no light, no seats, no lavatories, and insufficient numbers even of these; or railway arches and basements that gave an impression of safety, but had only a few inches of brick overhead, or were rotten shells of buildings with thin roofs and floors. In our borough we were well provided as regards numbers; there were almost sufficient for the night population, and they were reasonably safe, some being reinforced basements under fairly strong buildings, others being sunk just below ground level with concrete walls and ceilings. In my Post area we had two capacious shelters under business firms, which held three or four hundred, also fifteen small sub-surface concrete ones in which fifty people could sit upright on narrow wooden benches along the wall. But they were poorly ventilated, and only two out of the nine that came in my province could pretend to be dry. Some leaked through the roof, and umbrellas had to be used; in others the mouth of the sump-hole near the door had been made higher than the floor, and on rainy nights it invariably overflowed to a depth of two inches at one end of the shelter, decreasing to a quarter of an inch at the other, and rheumaticky old ladies had to sit upright on their benches for six to twelve hours on end, with their feet propped on a couple of bricks. Four or five times during the night we used to go round with a saucepan and bucket baling out the stinking water; as soon as Number 9 was reached, Number 1 was full again. It was hard, wet, and smelly work. Some of the shelterers took it too much for granted that this was part of the warden's job. I 'struck' one night. There were at least eight men under fifty, and four lads of sixteen or seventeen in the shelter, and I downed tools, saying that I wouldn't do any more unless they lent a hand themselves. I considered that a mean should be struck between helping people and inducing them to help themselves.

Every week, sometimes twice a week, with monotonous regularity, we reported an inch of water in such and such shelters. Once the contractor's engineer came and suggested that it was all due to the sweating of the concrete. Nothing else was done, until long after the raiding ceased.

But if conditions in many of our shelters were bad, in some other districts they were incredible. They belonged more properly to the days of a hundred years ago than to the twentieth century. To-day, it is admitted that the provision of a certain amount of medical supervision, and tolerable living conditions, are necessary for production and domestic peace. It is, perhaps, understandable that sleeping accommodation was not provided. It had, apparently, not occurred to the Government that raiding might be continuous throughout the night. One can say that it should have done so, as it certainly occurred to many ordinary citizens, at least by the time of Denmark's invasion. But the fact remains that it did not. The millions of bunks needed could hardly have been provided more quickly than they were, once the need for them was belatedly realised.

Again, the Government's argument that it was impossible to provide safety from direct, or very close, hits for the whole population was also tenable, if unpopular; and this is not the place to go into the relative strengths of the various types of shelter.

But lavatories—lighting—ventilation! For the lack of these there can be no excuse. Even if a raid is only going to last an hour, it is still frightening, and a lavatory is essential. There cannot be any argument about it. I have seen shelters which were built over the gutter, and this was left unscreened to run across the middle of the floor. In our area we were well off. There were chemical closets usually partially screened by a canvas curtain. But even so, the supervision of the cleaning of these was not adequate. Sometimes they would be left untended for days on end, and would overflow on to the floor. On one of these occasions, with difficulty, we moved the offending article outside. We had already reported it the night before. In the morning the police said that it could not stand outside in the public gaze; we said that still less could it stand inside under the public's nose. Even a regulation-minded police-sergeant could see the force of this argument, and a report went from the Station to the Town Hall and had the desired effect.

Then the question of lights. I have been told by wardens that, for the first two months, shelters in some boroughs had no light at all. We had one hurricane lamp for about fifty people. How often in the small hours, if the raid had started early, there would be a wail of 'Warden! Warden! The light's gone out!' and children would wake up and howl, women grow nervous, and the men would swear. It was expecting altogether too much of people's nerves to ask them to sit through a raid in the dark. That one paraffin lamp also provided the only heating that there was in those days. It was bitterly cold that winter, and naturally, therefore, the door was kept shut. Some of the bigger shelters had ventilation pipes, but the smaller ones that held fifty people had only the door. In some, the atmosphere of dank concrete, of stagnant air, the inevitable smell of bodies, the stench of the chemical closets was indescribable. More than once I had to stop a conversation abruptly and go outside to avoid being sick. It is begging the question to say that they must have been dirty people. Cleanliness is almost entirely dependent on the provision of material facilities. Few of us would be as clean as we are if water were not laid on. Big stores and hotels in the West End provided some grand shelters, complete with amenities; but apart from these, ours were, in the early days, among the best in London.

Why did people tolerate such conditions? After improvements were made, newspaper columnists speculated on this question. Was it stupidity, or was it courageous endurance? Probably there was a little of each, but the main reason was fear. If you live in an old and rickety house that trembles at a passing bus, or at the top of a block of flats; if you have children, or are old and slow in moving; or if you were simply brought up to be nervous and uncontrolled—you are justified in being afraid. There are too many factors on the debit side for you to be able to say, 'Oh, well—let's take a chance.'

It was fear that stirred usually docile men and women to storm the forbidden tubes with sufficient determination to succeed. Often, there were angry, violent scenes, but the police and the porters could not, and would not, turn the invaders out. The authorities had to give way. Every afternoon, about four o'clock, a pathetic procession started in every street. Old men and women, young women with children, emerged from their doors, all carrying mountainous bundles of bedding. They unrolled them on the platforms, in the passages, even on the escalators and stairways. Once there, the relief from the danger upstairs was so great that they tolerated almost obscene conditions, rather than risk being turned out again for making further demands. Some newspapers appeared outraged at the number of able-bodied men who 'went below.' But in their case the need for rest was at least as great as the desire for safety. It is not at all the same thing to manage an office from 10 a.m. onwards, as to leave at 6 a.m. for a heavy and monotonous day's work on a machine, after a whole night spent sitting on a bench, with nowhere for your head except your own chest, or your neighbour's shoulder.

In the larger Underground stations sheer force of numbers, and the leadership of a few stalwarts, compelled the provision of lavatories. But in the ordinary public shelters the numbers were not so large, and also there was no station master on the spot to receive demands, and be made to feel uncomfortable and nervous. Men could not take time off work in order to protest to the Local Authority before it finished work at 5 p.m. In any case, protests are not likely to be effective when there is no threat that can be used as a bargaining weapon. When you can say, 'If you don't do this, I won't work for you,' there is some hope of success. But who was going to care if

Above: Off to the Shelter, *Edward Ardizzone*
Below: Sleeping in a Shelter, *Edward Ardizzone*

shelterers said, 'If you don't provide decent facilities, we won't use your shelters'? Once, nine or ten of our shelters sent their marshals and leading members to the Town Hall, with a request that something be done about the water and the closets. They told me about it in the evening. 'But nothing will come of it, Miss—you see.' And they were right, nothing did—unless improvements ordered ten months later can be called something.

Locally, after the first few nights, people began to select the company they preferred, and very quickly each of our shelters developed a distinct character of its own, which was dependent to a large extent on the shelter marshal. Mrs. Barker, in charge of No. 2, brought down her gramophone, and her shelter was noisy and gay. With a lusty voice she led the singing, and kept it up till three or four in the morning if it was a noisy night. When a bomb burst within earshot she roared into 'Roll out the barrel' with admirable gusto. The next shelter was in the charge of a retired post office worker with silver white hair, and they were all very nervous and quiet: they even complained about Mrs. Barker's gramophone, saying that the German pilots overhead would hear the noise and drop a bomb on them all! The younger people congregated in the next one, and it became known as the courting shelter. Those in the main road had a more casual population, and that necessarily meant a percentage of drunks and fights. In the large shelter near the railway station there were frequent raucous brawls; twice, women were delivered of children; and drunken adolescents gambled, and upset the chemical closets, and indulged in every form of anti-social behaviour.

An enormous amount depended on the shelter marshal. If he or she was weak or officious there would always be trouble. Naturally, there were many such: they had volunteered for the job because it gave them relative immunity from the hazards above ground, or because they wanted to be in a superior position to their neighbours. But there were many more who controlled their shelters admirably. They were good-tempered and patient, they settled disputes with firmness, and went to considerable trouble on behalf of their charges. Male and female marshals would go back to their houses several times during the night, while the raids were on, and make great jugs of tea to be handed round. Some showed initiative in entertainment, or took first-aid courses, and set up small medical aid posts

Good spirits in Holborn Underground station

in one of the bays. In these cases a healthy community spirit grew up very quickly. Many, in fact, became so attached to this communal life that it was difficult to persuade them to move even a year after the blitzes had stopped.

Then there were the Andersons. The Government issued a spate of propaganda in their favour; the public covered them with abuse. Very many were unused. There can be little doubt, now, that they gave a considerable degree of safety, and stood up to ferocious blast from bombs particularly well, as they were below the surface. But many of them were uninhabitable owing to damp. The one in my own garden accumulated six inches of water the day that the workmen left it. It had risen to two feet six three days later, and remained at that level ever since. No amount of baling could make any difference. Secondly, the noise was appalling; the crack of the guns, and the whine and crash of bombs burst through the narrow opening, and reverberated in the confined space within: a loud explosion outside became ear-splitting inside an Anderson. Many found that they could not sleep in them, and lack of rest is as dangerous to morale as fear of bombs. Thirdly, the fact of being in large shelters with a number of neighbours and strangers forced some, who would otherwise have let their nerves get the upper hand of them, at least to keep up appearances. Bravery is often difficult to assess at its real value. Many brave actions have been carried out almost unconsciously, some have been foolhardy and lucky. But the ability to keep up appearances is all-important. Collective security achieved a reality in the shelters that it had never gained in European affairs.

Some insisted on staying in their houses. From a casualty and labour point of view it was not a particularly good thing. If the house should get hit it would mean more digging, and more uncertainty. But in alarming situations such as raids, people must be allowed to follow their fancy to a certain extent. Big Edith of 'the flats' was a case in point. She was not mobile, as she was well over fifty, was nearly blind, and weighed fourteen or fifteen stone. But, 'No,' she said, 'I'm staying 'ere, and if the block comes down, I'll sail down with it. You don't see me trying to get through them hatchets (emergency escape hatches) in the shelters.' And Fred, her husband, who had no more substance than a suit of clothes suspended on a coathanger, so thin was he, had willy-nilly to stay with

Some preferred to take the risks of staying at home

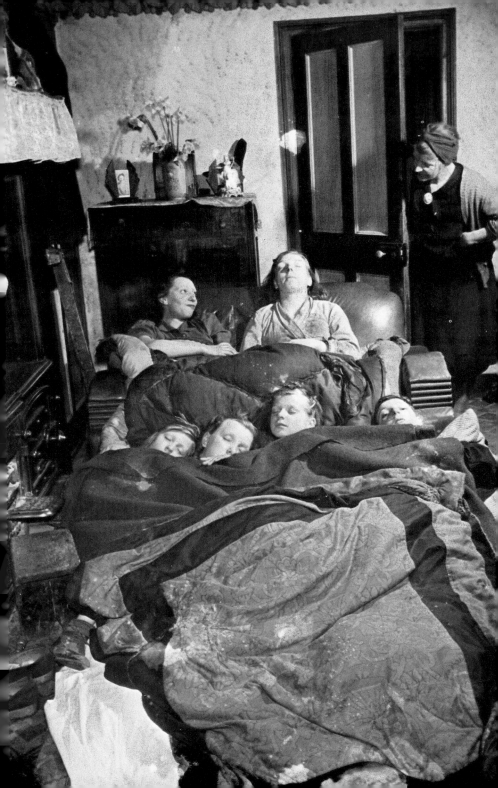

her. She had sufficient determination to lead an army, and she wasn't 'going to let *her* dinner spoil for no 'Itler.'

The number of old men and women in shelters was far too great. They ought to have been evacuated to the country, but they refused to go. Before the war it was commonly assumed that it was the villager, or at least the countryman, who was most deeply rooted to his home. One knew that the Cockney was seldom happy for long, away from London, but one had not realised how extraordinarily devoted he was, not only to London as a whole, not even to his borough area, but to his actual street. I tried to persuade an old lady of over eighty to apply to the evacuation office. She had been 'bombed out' utterly and completely, and had no possessions except the clothes she had been wearing. She lived by herself, and it would have been a simple matter to arrange for her evacuation. But, in common with very many others, she believed that her 10s. a week pension could only be paid to her at her local post office, and that if she went away she would literally starve, or have to live on 'charity.' I tried to persuade her that this was not the case; I offered to go with her to the post office and the Town Hall, but when I had won that point she said, 'But, Miss, I couldn't leave London.' She told me that she had a daughter and two sons living in the adjoining borough or in N. London—relatively a safe area—and that they had asked her to go to them. But, 'Oh no, I couldn't live anywhere else but Amwell Street, Miss.' Amwell Street was 'flat,' and would not be rebuilt for some years, but I left her searching for a room just round the corner, so that she would be on the spot when rebuilding should start.

This fear of losing their pension allowances, or post office savings, was very great. It may sound absurd to those who have bank balances, but it was very real to those who had not, and no amount of argument would shake it, as a rule. The blind, the crippled, and the very old would say, 'Yes, Miss; thank you, Miss; I'll go, Miss,' but they never went. They were a liability to us, particularly at the start of each raid; but since they would not be evacuated, the wardens were very considerate of them. Even the toughest, who had spent their whole lives among race-course gangs, generally had their 'specials' whom they carried or helped down to their shelter immediately the siren went.

It is difficult to determine whether the bombing was more

alarming for these old ones than for the young. Neither had any idea what it was all about; they had never heard of Poland before the war, and Fascism was, at most, a matter of that wicked beast Hitler, who was trying to blow us up, or murder us all in our beds. The first time that we found an undamaged incendiary bomb—or incidental bomb as they were called locally—we showed it in several of the shelters, and found that a great number had thought that all bombs were round, with a stick jutting out of the top, like those of Guy Fawkes's day. I strongly suspected also that the common phrase 'you're only hit by one with your name on it' was, in some cases, backed by a miraculous faith that some Ruhr munitions worker had actually stamped 'Mrs. Perkins, 16 Tichbourn Street,' on his handiwork.

Ignorance, however, is a certain protection. It was with the children; the vast majority did not seem to be much affected. I have seen some children who would stand shivering and sweating in a shelter, and no amount of coaxing would induce them to utter a word. But most of them slept soundly, and only showed a healthy excitement. Every morning one was besieged by crowds of small boys and girls: 'Got any shrapnel, Miss? Billy got a shell cap yesterday—give me one, Miss.' Collecting shrapnel and bits of bombs was more the rage than the vanished cigarette card had been.

Psychologists have stated that the nervous complaints of children due to evacuation and separation from home have been more numerous than those due to bombing. That might be true of children who lived in Hampstead or Kensington, which did not get hit extensively or continuously; but it is hard to believe that anything could have a more serious effect on a child's stability than to feel the earth itself heave, and the shelter rock to and fro, or, worse, to have the whole house crash down upon him.

Whatever deleterious effects might develop later, their spirits at the time were not affected, and the normal propensity for destructiveness was vastly increased. The devastation around them gave them all the greater scope. It was possible to have wonderful wars amongst the débris, and in the battered and abandoned basements. Bricks made excellent hand grenades, and if a stray passer-by received one of these grenades it just made the war so much the more modern and realistic. Empty derelict houses offered endless opportunities for explorers and pirates, however unsafe they were.

Barriers, notices, police and wardens could not keep them out. The larger ones of twelve or thirteen played at being demolition workers, if it could be called playing. Once or twice there were disastrous results.

In one shelter where, later, we cleared a bay of its bunks to make a recreation room, the children themselves helped with the clearance, carefully counted the nuts and bolts, and behaved in exemplary fashion. The next night, their games became distinctly noisy, and some women protested with vigour. The children retaliated by pouring water down the ventilation pipes on to the bunks below; the women, thereupon, made use of two broomsticks, and the children capped that by resorting to the iron bunk poles. Peace was, with difficulty, finally restored, but the next morning the children had the final word. They threw all the precious nuts and bolts through the windows of the houses. And the ringleader of it all was a chubby little person called Pozzie, who would always proudly announce that he was 'eleven, rising twelve.'

The new community life in shelters had its good points. Many, who had never given a thought to anyone outside their own family

circle, became more considerate and helpful, and less selfish. But at first there was a danger of epidemics on a colossal scale. In our area we suggested to the shelterers that they and we should club together and buy disinfectant sprays. It was the least we could do, and I believe it happened in other boroughs also. Before October ended, however, orders were issued that larger shelters must have medical supervision, bunks, chemical closets at least, running water and canteens.

Owing to the energy of hundreds of nurses and doctors, a good health service was quickly got going. We had several cases of measles or scarlet fever, yet they never spread to the other occupants. In fact, the health of the poorer members of the community was actually improved. Other ailments than infectious diseases were noticed, and treated, more quickly than would have been the case in individual homes. Even the old, who were suffering from chronic complaints, learned where they could get treatment. Impetigo was checked. The only thing that grew rampant was scabies. Panel doctors often advised simple applications of sulphur, whereas there was a thoroughly effective and quick treatment provided by the borough, free. In many shelters, old and young would sit scratching their fingers interminably.

The newly-built shelters were, as a rule, free of bugs and lice. But those in the basements of old buildings frequently swarmed with them. Before the war, the space had often been used as a store-room, or dump, and however many times they were fumigated, the evil little creatures crawled out again. Sometimes they were not reported for two or three weeks, until their mass formations were inescapable, because the first persons to notice them did not say anything, fearing that they would be accused of having brought them in, in their bedding.

Personally, as I did not have to sleep among them, I did not have so great an objection to the bugs as the lice. At least you could see the former and squash them, despite the filthy smell. But the several varieties of lice I found literally horrifying, and considered myself very lucky that I only picked some up once. They were usually brought in by tramps of no fixed abode, who were saving the shilling that a Salvation Army hostel would have cost them, or by others who, for various reasons, were on the move. We had, of course, authority to turn out a lousy person, if he or she refused to go and get cleansed. But one needed actual evidence. One could not take merely the word of the 'regulars.' They resented an intruder, and their statements might have no more validity than a small boy's assertion that Perkins minor did not wash behind his ears. It was to be hoped that in the rebuilding of London these disgusting pests would be treated as a major public enemy, instead of being deplored as one of the inevitable misfortunes of the poor. No amount of soap or energy can keep you clean, if you have to live in a bug-ridden building.

The larger shelters of London organised recreation fairly early. Christmas gave the idea a start, and London Region and many Local Authorities instituted Shelter Welfare Officers, and Shelter Committees. Such work was, of course, easier when there was considerable space, and when the population was chiefly skilled or regular factory workers. Libraries, concerts, lectures and play centres for the children were started, and thrived. It was an admirable opportunity for truly democratic organisation. For the first time, on a large scale, the Englishman left the decaying and often infested home, which is euphemistically called his castle, and mixed with his fellows. There was opportunity for improving the education of the children, widening the interests of the adults, and generally inculcating an understanding of the war, and the need for communal effort.

In our borough, however, no such work was organised until several months after the blitzes had ceased. Our shelters were, many of them, underground labyrinths, divided into innumerable small bays. This made them safer than the spacious variety, but it made entertainment difficult. Yet something could have been done. Before the war there had been loud and justifiable complaints that the public was too apathetic to vote or take an interest in local government. In the shelters, where a consciousness of collective responsibility was beginning to develop, there were far better opportunities for discussion than in the shopping queue, on the street corner, or in the public-house. It does not require much imagination to think of ways by which the Local Authority, by the speedy provision of decent conditions, physical and mental, through hygienic measures, entertainment and lectures, could have galvanised popular feeling, and made democracy a reality. It may have been due to stupidity or blindness on the part of the officials, but I am inclined to think that it was due to a preference for ruling by decree. Genuine democracy needs not only more organisation and effort than rule by a caucus of small officials, but also a new approach, of which many of these were regrettably incapable. During the raids almost the whole population went to shelter, and the majority to the public ones. If the marshals had been encouraged officially to act as public organisers, and to get shelter committees elected, much would have been achieved. But the Town Hall gave the impression that they thought anything in the nature of a shelter committee was a Communist invention, until a circular from London Region, much later, categorically stated that they were a good thing.

When the raids were over, the more rational and able-bodied members of the public ceased to use the shelters, and in the main, the occupants who continued to sleep there each night were the very old, the families with small children, and the adolescents who came to use the canteens where such had been installed. The old ladies did not want to do anything. They did not want to knit, they were not able to read; they were momentarily interested in a picture paper when such a thing was available, and they liked an occasional sing-song.

In this post-raid period shelters soon divided into quiet and noisy ones, and in the latter we sometimes managed to hold dances. Boys and girls and small children jitterbugged with zest and skill to the deafening strains of a piano-accordian and mouth-organ. Every now and then there would be a call for 'Knees up, Mother Brown,' and enormous ladies who bounced and swayed in all directions, lame old gentlemen with sticks, and thin meagre little women, who hardly opened their mouths in the ordinary way, would twirl and scream, and bob up and down in a whirl of excitement. Hats and toques wriggled into perilous and drunken positions over one eye, buttons and pins burst, shawls got entangled, till the instruments were drowned by the panting, gasping screams.

Film shows were popular with both children and adults, and provided an excellent means of instruction as well as entertainment. There was always risk of a riot if the projector broke down, as 16 mm projectors so often will. Flanagan and Allen, Charlie Chaplin, and a Russian 'short' called 'Three in a Shell-hole' were the favourites, and they got them sandwiched between more educational documentaries. Unfortunately these favourites were not on any free list, and so, although it was not, strictly speaking, allowed, we took a collection of a penny per head, or a halfpenny if you hadn't got a penny. Of course, if you hadn't got a halfpenny either, you got in just the same; but nearly all the children produced a coin of some sort, except crack business men like Pozzie, who on every occasion had a long and circumstantial story of how he had 'lost' his.

They were all sound films, but they might just as well have been silent for all you could ever hear of the dialogue or commentary. 'Charlie' and 'Three in a Shell-hole' produced cheers fit to split the concrete—'Hooray, the Roosians—Boo the Nazzies—Hooray—Boo!' One child laughed wildly as one of the Russian soldiers staggered, hit in the knee, but was immediately quelled by a high-pitched squeal above the din, from a more knowledgeable small boy, 'Shut up, you silly! It's a Roosian!' Not one word of the dialogue could be heard, and not one word of the commentary on an old 'Charlie'; but the suggestion of having silent films was immediately howled down.

Concerts were as popular as film shows. Local talent—more local than talented—was preferred to that of visitors. Occasionally someone would be found with the makings of the traditional music-hall comedian, but the singing——! When the Board of Directors of the BBC arrives at the pearly gates of heaven, and asks for admission on the grounds of having spread a knowledge of music, most divine of the arts, among a no longer musical people, St. Peter will sadly shake his respectable grey locks and say, 'Ah, but where are all the tattered vocal chords of those whom you encouraged to croak and scream and croon instead of singing? No, gentlemen, your microphones, and the raucous noises you have taught people to make through them, belong downstairs with our infernal friend. You have not provided us with one recruit who could produce a decent hallelujah!'

The microphone and the talent-spotting competition have ruined many possible voices, and have made many sing who would have done far better to have remained silent. Blondes of seventeen would distort their faces and their voices if there was a microphone; without one, they could do nothing even in a small space. One girl, with a small but true voice, never got much applause because she sang without the modern affectations. Everybody knew by heart the songs that the radio kept plugging, night after night, in almost every programme. Little girls of six would undulate their bodies in suggestive contortions, ogle the audience with their infants' eyes, and sing about the breasts and hips that they did not yet possess. Sometimes there would be a storm of shushing, and when that died down you would be aware of a tiny little squeak coming from a completely invisible (since there was no platform) performer, aged two or three.

Classical music was as popular as the new songs. But in these circumstances classical does not mean Bach or Schubert: it refers to 'My Irish Rose' or 'Two Lovely Black Eyes,' as opposed to the more racy tunes such as 'The Sailor with the Navy Blue Eyes' and 'Oh, Johnny.'

Tap dancing was another travesty of an art. As done by Fred Astaire, tap dancing is fascinating to watch, and as skilled as ballet or other forms of dancing. But it is much too easy to jig up and down while making tapping noises with the feet, and without any rhythmical movement of the body. However, although all the canons of artistic taste were shockingly violated, the concerts were much enjoyed; and let that be their excuse.

Christmas parties made extremely hot work, but were really enjoyable. Parents and residents in the street or square concerned clubbed together with cash, or half a pot of jam here, and a bit of margarine there, to provide a tea for the children. ('Bring your own cup.') There were singing and dancing and a film. Some of the wardens made toys from débris wood. We scrounged the paint, and a number of snappy trucks, tanks, and boats were turned out. The pleasure they gave was immeasurable.

On one occasion, when it had been firmly decided that the party should be for the twenty children of that shelter only, I arrived with the correct number of toys in a sack, only to find that the loud-mouthed but soft-hearted Mrs. Thompson, who ran the canteen, had admitted eighty. There was no escape, and I could not hide the inadequate sackful, as I had been spotted long before I reached the entrance. The remainder of my progress was hampered by children clinging to my clothes, hanging round my neck, standing on my feet. I despaired of ever effecting a distribution without a riot from the sixty toyless ones. We decided on a lucky ticket system.

But a shelter is not a school, nor have parents the authority or sense of teachers. And even if, after considerable bellowing, you can get some sort of queue formed, you cannot prevent some small gentlemen crawling through ventilation pipes, or inter-bay hatch-ways, to gain a wrongfully advanced place in the line. I started the distribution with a clear space round me maintained by other wardens. But when I produced a pink-spotted wooden horse that you could sit on, not all the wardens of the borough could have held the mass assault that ensued. Nevertheless, we avoided any fights, and there was not much wailing, as we managed to find a three-penny bit each for the unlucky ones. The only casualty was my voice. The boys dashed off to try their boats in the static water tank nearby, and came back wet, announcing haughtily that the aircraft carriers were not really seaworthy.

On another occasion the WVS provided a four-foot long cracker with small toys inside. The shelter concerned was better controlled by its marshal, and was in a less poor quarter. All the children had shiny faces and wet, smooth hair; some had shiny party frocks. I hid the cracker till late in the proceedings, hoping that they would be tired by then. We collected the children under ten. There were too many, so we reduced it to those under eight. I produced the cracker. With piercing squeals all the little tots fell on it, and me, like tigers. If I had not been wearing a leather jacket, I doubt if I should have retained my shirt. Within thirty seconds there was not a shred of cracker left.

When there was money left over from the collections we distri-buted it among the children at threepence or sixpence each, or whatever it would run to. Pozzie, of course, 'lost' his sixpence within half an hour, hoping for another one. The wardens helped a great deal on these occasions and, almost without being asked, turned up to maintain a modicum of decorum. I remember finding one very dour, almost grim, woman warden hopping solemnly round and round a side bay with fifteen toddlers she had rescued from being crushed and battered by the older dancers in the main bay. Parents were very feckless with their infants.

The LCC and the Save the Children Fund provided volunteers to run play centres. These valiant women turned up regularly after their day's work to face a howling stampede of twenty to eighty children, scrambling and squealing for coloured chalks, and puzzles and games. After the first ten minutes, relative order was achieved, and for two hours the children were kept happy and busy. Only the teachers with a sense of humour, as well as kindliness, survived. One lady told me, on her first visit, that she 'loved little children' and was delighted to come and help. I was dubious, as she was obviously expecting the docility of a refined kindergarten. When I went down the shelter an hour later she was sitting hopelessly on a bench. 'But these aren't children,' she wailed. 'They're *animals*.'

One useful device was to form a committee of the children themselves, and ensure that at least two of the inevitable tough gang were on it. It may have smacked of Darlanism, but in this case the object was to preserve peace, and it worked. The methods may not always have been exactly constitutional. I arrived once to find 'committee-man' Sammy Hutton (aged nine) disputing with a wiry little seven-year-old as to which of them should have the meccano box next. 'You're not committee—you're only ordinary—you can't have it,' and bosh, down came the box on the seven-year-old's head. 'Committee-man' Sammy was regarded, even by the locality, as certain of a scholarship to Borstal. But when put in charge of the library of fifteen books, he did not lose or 'fiddle' one, and kept the borrowers strictly to their time limit.

Some parents were exasperating. When they wanted to go out they turned their children into the streets to get into all sorts of trouble and danger, and yet would refuse permission for them to go to the play centre, because it was three streets away. But one good result of the war is the increase in these play centres. In our borough, where there were none before, there are now four large and thriving centres, catering for more than a hundred children each, and running boxing, carpentry, sewing classes, and most indoor games, after school hours. Even if the average city home were less cramped and more hygienic than it is, and the parents less tired and more reasonable, this is still an essential part of a good educational system, and in those days needed much wider development.

Official policy on shelters was sometimes obscure. Provision of recreation and instruction was properly authorised even after raiding had stopped, but at the same time the Ministry declared that this recreation must not be so attractive as to induce people to stay in, or visit, shelters who might otherwise remain at home. Yet, on the whole, shelter life was better than that in many homes. The air was no worse, medical attention was received more speedily; it was possible to help and control the children and adolescents to a certain extent; the adults began to realise that they were members of a community, and tempers and selfishness were more controlled. For years, the ordinary man, or woman, had been inaccessible in his or her back street. Was not the new community life an opportunity which should have been utilised and developed?

The regular users gave little trouble. What trouble there was, was caused chiefly by visiting gangs of lads from neighbouring areas, who organised raids, or by the sudden influx due to an occasional alert in the long months of quiet. On one of the latter occasions there was a grand rumpus, including a prime example of Marx Brothers' wit. The siren wailed at 10.15 one Saturday night, when Mrs. Magg and her cronies were celebrating young Magg's first leave from the army, in the local. Young Magg was a weedy youth, but the ladies were mountains of strength. The whole party adjourned from the local to the shelter, complete with ample means for continued celebration. On arrival, they found that the bay which they had always occupied during the raids had been cleared of its bunks to make a recreation space for the children. There were one hundred and sixty-three other bunks vacant and available—but these would not do. An unholy row started. Wardens came down and tried to restore peace; other officials arrived, and paled before the flow of language and the brandished bottles. Finally came the fat little mayor. With dignity he inquired what all this was about. Mrs. Magg swung round, 'Who the bleedin' 'ell are you?' she shouted. 'My good woman, I'm the Mayor.' 'I don't care if you're the effin' 'orse,' came the reply, 'I want my bleedin' bunk.'

"My good woman, I'm the Mayor."

Searching the rubble in Ducket Street, Stepney

6

Post 13

By December 1940 I decided to become a full-time warden. I was already putting in more than the requisite number of hours and, more important, any other work that I could get entailed leaving London, which, in the circumstances, I was not prepared to do. I therefore applied to be paid the magnificent sum of £2 5s. a week.

The Town Hall, however, had objections. First, they said they did not want any more women; then, when that argument was disposed of, they said they would not employ married women, and asked me why I wanted to work when I was married. At length, after four or five weeks, they agreed to appoint me, but said that I must go to Post 13 at the other end of the borough. This was annoying, as I had made several friends on Post 2, and one's company during raids is a very important matter. If your partner shows his nervousness it is infectious, and, on the other hand, a too brazen nonchalance is irritating and gives you an inferiority complex. B.B. never got excited, yet never pretended that he liked it, and we got on very well together. In addition, I now knew the area and the population.

I made enquiries as to what '13' was like. Apart from jokes about its number, what I learned was not encouraging. They were considered the toughest set of wardens in the borough. Once, they had had a woman on the strength, but she had left months ago. They did not like women. And they had had by far the heaviest fall of bombs in the neighbourhood, half the area being completely devastated. It was part of a district which, according to an official account, 'remains to-day perhaps the largest area of continuous air-raid desolation in all Britain.'*

I went along to see for myself. As soon as one approached, one was met by a strong, acrid smell of burning cardboard, and filthy rubble. Many of the ruined shells of buildings still had hoses playing

*This does not mean that ours was the most heavily *bombed* borough. Poplar and Bermondsey would probably hold the record for that.

on the débris, although it was two weeks since the last raid. The branches were fixed, and the water splashed down in a desultory manner all day, and all night. Some of them were still smouldering four weeks later. I do not think that, even at that time, there was a single street without some damage, and many of them were not there at all. Seventy per cent of the damage had been caused by the City fire, although they had had a considerable number of high explosives and oil bombs dropped on the area before that. But I had missed that most spectacular raid of all by catching the infantile disease of chicken-pox.

It is no exaggeration to say that half of the damage that night could have been prevented, had the business firms had sufficient sense of responsibility to employ fire-watchers. For a hundred years the City had been marked as a danger area for fire, and yet nothing had been done. What fire-watchers there were, worked heroically, and often controlled dozens of incendiary bombs in their buildings, only to be forced to abandon them to their fate, because the premises next door had been locked and barred with steel shutters. It can almost be considered a miracle that the weather changed, and the Germans could not follow up the incendiaries with high explosive. Had they done so, the death-roll would have been enormous, as the wardens' chief job that night had been to move three or four hundred people at a time from one shelter to another, as each in turn became too hot to be tenable. As it was, civilian casualties in our area were nil. It was the firemen who lost their lives—crushed and burnt—when towering walls crashed down on them.

The Wardens' Post was a wooden shack in the centre of Moorgate. I learnt later that it had lost its roof on the night of the big fire. I was used to a basement, and this looked very flimsy to me. As a general prospect, it was not cheering. I was alarmed and depressed.

I duly reported at 20 hours that evening, very apprehensive, and very shy. Six or seven wardens were sitting in the hut. Two looked up for a moment from a game of cards, but nobody said anything, and the game was resumed. I muttered that I was the new warden and asked which was Mr. Harding, the Post Warden. A stocky, square-faced chap reading the paper said, 'Me,' and continued to read the paper. Feeling foolish standing up, I sat on the edge of the table, since all the chairs were occupied. Still nobody said anything, so I also made a pretence of reading the paper.

After minutes that felt like half an hour, Harding said, 'Well, I suppose we had better settle your day off.' I said that I liked Sunday, but presumed that so did everyone else. Apparently not—one man liked Wednesdays because of the Dogs, another Fridays because he did a job with a lorry on that day, and so on, and I got my Sunday. Harding went on, 'We do days or nights here; none of that swapping about. I suppose you want days.' I said that I would rather do nights, if it was all the same to him. He seemed a little surprised, but said, 'Oh yes,' and then added, 'Sign the book, and then you'd better clear off, and report to-morrow at 20 hours. If you like to come along in the morning, I'll show you the shelters.' Altogether I felt extremely despondent, and far less welcome than on my first day at boarding school. I went back to my old Post, and had some beer with B.B. to cheer myself up. He was very sympathetic, and Jim Mackin, the Post Warden, said he would do his best to get me back there.

The next morning I went down to '13.' It was raining: the smell was abominable, and it looked more desolate than ever. Harding was there and we started off on a tour of the district. Ropemaker

Street was roped off, and the barricade was covered with sixty or seventy shabby little notices written in ink or indelible pencil, saying that such-and-such a firm had moved to another address. The ink and the pencil had run in the rain, and they looked very bedraggled. This street had been one of tall, though old-fashioned, office buildings. Not one was left; there were only heaps of charred rubble and bricks. At the far end, in solitary dinginess, a public-house was still standing. Despite the fact that it was not much damaged, it was boarded up—its roof was still there, but its customers had all gone. The next street was only a footpath between piles of bricks and beams, and for acres on each side there was complete devastation. The area had been thickly covered with factories, and warehouses, and office buildings; now, it was a fantastic tangle of girders—girders a foot thick, twisted and curled like a child's hair-ribbon.

During raids this was one of the most impressive sights I have seen. Occasional jagged walls were still standing, one factory building was almost intact, but was split down the middle, each half leaning

Devastation, 1941: City, Twisted Girders, *Graham Sutherland*   77

outwards at a perilous angle, and only held together by a gimcrack little iron footbridge on the roof. One expected every burst of gunfire to bring it toppling down. We always had a large number of fires in our area, and silhouetted against the red, and sometimes greenish or white, firelight, this chaotic tangle of ruins dwarfed Pompeii, with its Vesuvius, into insignificance. Nothing was left. The heart of the largest city in the world was a wilderness. Here and there, desultory trails of smoke curled up; the pigeons had deserted it, no gulls circled over it, the only inhabitants were occasional, scurrying rats. Within a year, groundsel and desiccated willow-herb were growing where the hallways of world-famous firms had stood.

In the middle of this annihilation a sub-surface shelter was still intact; the occupants had had to be evacuated when the fire above grew too hot, but none had been hurt. We made a detour as there was an unexploded bomb ahead of us, and climbed over piles fifteen feet high of bricks, beams, girders, and rubble till we reached the less ruined part. This consisted, in the main, of blocks of grey, barrack-like Peabody flats—two rooms and no bath. About one in every three was damaged, and hardly any had any windows, but the loss of life had been small. After the attack on the docks, this area had been one of the first to suffer heavy bombing, so that the population quickly developed a healthy respect for the bombs and, with few exceptions, all went to shelter.

At night it was a dead city. The few small shops were barred and shuttered, and the blocks of flats were deserted. If there was no gunfire or drone of planes, it was quieter than the countryside. Even in an open field, the soughing of a tree in the breeze, the rustle of a rat in a hedge, or the wheeze of a cow, can still be heard. But here the silence was almost tangible—a literally dead silence, in which there was no life. It was difficult to believe that this was London, whose daily uproar never sank below a steady rumble, even in the small hours. After 10.30 p.m., when the public-houses turned out the few hardy regulars, the silence was complete, only broken occasionally by the echoing footsteps of a warden, or policeman, on patrol. All the population was underground. When the silence grew overpowering, we went down into a shelter to reassure ourselves that there still was some life in this deserted city. The shelters were much larger than those I had been used to, and would all hold three or four hundred at least. But they seemed drier, and were certainly better ventilated, and several had just had bunks installed in place of the benches.

We turned through an alley, and into a large courtyard enclosed on all sides by the backs of office buildings and blocks of flats. This was entirely filled with several score of surface shelters in rows. They were never used, as both the offices and the flats already had adequate sub-surface shelter accommodation, and the yard was not visible from the street. Six had been squashed by a bomb, four or five others had collapsed as a result of the attentions of the local children. Huddled together, they looked like the dwellings of some primitive tribe. They had been built according to Government order, by a contractor who used more sand than concrete, and were a shameful monument to both local and Government officialdom. The Government had allowed certain monies for building surface shelters, so the borough, which already had almost sufficient shelters, used that money to create a white elephant in an inaccessible and unfrequented spot. Despite shortage of labour and material, it was not apparently possible for the borough to reply that it did not need the whole of the grant, or for the Government to say that some of the money could be used for improvements to existing shelters; and so they rotted in a deserted backyard.

By this time I had completely lost my sense of direction; I knew that I should not be able to remember which shelter was which, and was appalled to think that I should have to make reports of damage to a district which I did not know at all, in which what distinguishing marks there might have been had gone, where even those streets that were left had had their name-plates blown away. After all, the first essential for a warden is to know his district thoroughly, so that reports can be accurate. And how was I ever to get any idea of the number of families in each vast block, or know whether the Harrisons and the Greenbaums went to one shelter or another? I felt that I should be of no use at all.

One effect of bombing, I believe fairly common among wardens, was that one came to believe that one was much safer in one's own area than anywhere else. On the occasions when I had been caught in the West End I had had a strong sense of insecurity, although the bombing was usually much lighter. On reaching one's own area one sighed with relief—here at least one knew which were the stronger doorways, where were the shelters, and, above all, that if one was

Overleaf: Destruction of part of a block of flats

missing for an hour someone would start a search. Here at '13' that feeling of insecurity returned; instead of modest two- or three-storey houses, there were vast seven-storey blocks to fall on me, and I felt that I could be buried for a week before anyone would be any the wiser. It was an irrational feeling, since small houses crumble easily, whereas a large block will only collapse entirely for the largest bombs. But one is not rational about being buried.

Meanwhile Harding was telling me about the other woman who had been at the Post—a Mrs. Thom. He said that she had been quite good, and had not lost her head; he had no particular objections to women himself, but some of the others had. I felt a little encouraged and suggested a drink. He looked a bit apprehensive, but agreed. When I ordered a bitter and an ale he grinned with relief, and explained that Mrs. Thom had only drunk port—if I liked bitter that was all right.

I was always curious to know what people had been or done before the war, but often it was most unwise to ask. Owing to the fact that race tracks, boxing rings, and similarly chancy means of livelihood closed down at the outbreak of war, there was a large percentage of bookie's touts, and even more parasitic professions, in the CD services, together with a mixed collection of workers in light industry, 'intellectuals,' opera singers, street traders, dog fanciers, etc. In the early days Control Rooms were crowded with chorus girls as telephonists, who often brightened considerably the lives of the permanent municipal employees. I met a warden called Bert O'Dwyer coming out of the 'Labour' one day, laughing all over his face. He told me that they had been very persistent in trying to find out what work he had done before the war. 'I told 'em, I said, "Look, miss, I never done a day's work in me life"; she said I must 'ave, what did I live on. "Me," I said, "me—I made money, I did, I never worked",' all with a mixture of pride and amusement as though he had built the Albert Memorial. However, although all of us would not, in the ordinary way, have been called worthy citizens, we had many who were first-class wardens, and despite no previous organisational experience, and without specific directions or active co-operation from the Town Hall, took charge of the public below and above ground, and rose to emergencies with courage and determination.

The fact that we were a very mixed lot made life more amusing.

82

Once, long after the blitzes, we played a cricket match against a 'posh' West End borough. Our 'tail' had never played much cricket other than the lamp-post variety, and only six of us knew that it was possible to hit a ball to the 'off,' while the other team contained two ex-county players and six double-barrelled names. It was a delightfully funny afternoon. At tea their captain, who looked like an ex-colonel, singled me out as the most likely conversationalist in the team, and kept asking me if I did not think cricket was 'so-good-for-the-men's-morale—what?,' while Tommy whistled for the waitress and called her Joycie, and little Johnnie Cope at mid-on let out a cheer when one of their batsmen was bowled off his chin.

It was obviously safe to ask Harding, however, what his work had been, and I found that he was an electrician. He read a great deal, and was at the moment in the middle of a history of the last war. I had been warned that he told you what he thought of you long before you had any desire to know, and he was often curt to the point of rudeness. Only once did I suffer personally from his tongue, when I arrived three-quarters of an hour late. But I had excruciating tooth-ache, had vainly tried the back-door of every chemist's shop on the way, and, though usually cowardly in verbal battles, that time I gave as good as I got. We both relapsed into gloomy silence, while nobody else made any comment. Half an hour later we each said simultaneously, 'What about a beer?'

There was no doubt as to who was 'guvnor' at the Post, but we needed a rather strong hand. Harding was a perfect 'bombing partner,' and we soon became firm friends. The Town Hall called him a Communist because he had made a fuss in the first few weeks about the shelters. Spacious, dry shelters under offices and private firms had been kept locked while people had to queue in the streets, long after the sirens had gone, before they could be squeezed into overcrowded public ones. He certainly was not shy of giving his opinions, but the Town Hall always called any person a Communist who expressed any ideas about anything, whether in fact they were, or not. Perhaps it was a compliment to the local Communist Party.

That night I felt much less alarmed by my new Post, although it was obvious that there was fairly strong resentment at having a 'b—— cow' dumped on them. Two openly resented it, two others reserved judgment, and the remaining three decided to make the best of a bad job. Within half an hour there were heavy apologies for a 'bloody.' I said 'not at all,' and explained that I had heard the word once or twice before, and in any case used it myself. Twenty minutes later there were much heavier apologies. I have never objected to anyone over the age of ten swearing, but apologies for it are irritating and ludicrous, so I decided that the only cure was to indulge myself, and there were no more excuses.

There was no alert that night, and after playing darts very badly for two hours I asked where the lavatory was, and was greeted with a roar of laughter. There wasn't one. I asked what Mrs. Thom had done. Nobody knew. But there were apparently four alternatives— (i) the railings; but against that there was a police post a little further along the street; (ii) the surface shelters eighty yards away, but these were not well looked after, were generally filthy, and usually occupied by courting couples; (iii) the public shelter further away, but this would mean marching right across the shelter in front of two hundred people whom I did not know at all, and then marching back again; (iv) the burial grounds. There, in a corner, was a tombstone with an inscription to a lady who had died in the late eighteenth century and had had more than a phenomenal number of gallons of water pumped out of her, before she could be got into a coffin. This was generally felt to be the most suitable. While I was away the siren went. I could hear the laughter in the hut caused by this, from the other side of the street. The atmosphere had unfrozen considerably, but I could not help feeling that the Town Hall did not show due consideration to the wants of its personnel. Two years later, another of our Posts was still having to use the floor of a ruined house next to them.

For the first two or three weeks that I was at '13' there was a comparative lull; there were raids each night, but nothing dropped in our area. I had learnt a number of the streets, and even the positions of such hydrants as were not buried, but I was not confident of my knowledge of the district, and could never disentangle the numbers, or rather letters, of the innumerable Council flats. The fact that many of them were referred to, more often than not, as Joe Daykin's place, or Harry's block, did not make it any easier. But I was beginning to know my companions.

One is apt to think of the London population as fluctuating or cosmopolitan, but in '13's' area this was far from true In the narrow streets, behind the imposing Edwardian office buildings, lived a community as closely knit together as that of any Cotswold village. All the wardens had been to the same local school, though at different times, and they knew the family history of nearly everyone in the neighbourhood. They, and their grandfathers in their day, had all played together as children, and been 'walloped' by a succession of heavy-handed schoolmasters. There were distinctions and different sets, and, as a classics man at Oxford is only on nodding terms with a modern languages man, so those who followed the steadier trades only nodded to those who had chosen the more rackety professions; but they knew all about them, and you never let the other lot down. Despite a deal of petty gossiping, particularly on the part of the women, there was an admirable loyalty. Old Bob H—— still got a very cool reception because, ten years before, he had informed on another race gang in order to get himself out of trouble.

There were eight of us on the night shift, and three voluntary wardens. One of these was seldom known to turn out in a raid; he was about 55, but had never grown any beard and his face was so puckered with wrinkles that he looked 90. For all practical purposes he was written off. For a heavy raid we were always likely to be understaffed. At Post 2 there had been more than twenty voluntary wardens as well as eleven full-timers, and about ten were women. This large number had one disadvantage, however, of creating 'sets' and cliques; and as women are usually more intolerant of other people's shortcomings, personal gossip was far too common At '13' if you had a grievance you had a row, a violent and abusive row, perhaps, that occasionally developed into a fight, but half an hour later it was over and forgotten. There were too few of us to take sides.

We had two Georges and two Bills. Both the Georges (the second one was more commonly called Blackie, or Georgie, or George the Second) had joined the Wardens' Service because they would not get called up for some time, and they thought that it was a good thing to do; Archie Hopkins, Arthur Purton and Stan Newman had joined because the race tracks closed, and they thought it would be easy money; Henry O'Leary had been temporarily out of work, and I don't think Frank Pilley or Bill No. 2 (Izzie) quite knew why they had joined.

Old Archibald Hopkins was in reality rather a dirty old man, but he was certainly a character. He came of generations of costers, and what he had not known about street trading, and how to get rid of the 'offs' on a Saturday night at the age of twelve, was not worth knowing. Since then he had done every race track in England —'er, um, beautiful country Newmarket, Barbara, beautiful country.' He prefaced every utterance with 'er-um' and a smack of his lips. He was not much help in a general conversation, as he always suffered from amnesia, and would side-track any argument for twenty minutes.

'Er rum, d'you know who I saw this morning?'

'No.'

'Oh—what's 'is name. Pushin' a barrer 'e was. Little feller.'

'Moustache?'

'Yus.'

'Brown 'air?'

'Yus.'

'Oh, Bertie Staggers.'

'Na, not 'im. Little feller. Used to keep a stall bottom of Bird Street.'

'Johnny Harris?'

'Na. Little feller—fancy me forgetting, now.'

'Moustache?'

'Yus.'

'Brown 'air?'

'Yus.'

'Bertie Staggers?'

'Na,' . . . And so it would go on.

Once when I was alone with Archie at the Post for an hour, he gave me a chaotic but fascinating account of his street when he was a 'nipper' in the 'nineties. Then it was a slum, and he painted a vivid picture of family life in one room—bawling women, neglected kids dodging school, given a penny by their mothers to get their dinner, and supplementing it by thieving from stalls as was expected of them. He was brought up on pease-pudding and lights. He told me how someone had, in the end, fixed it for his father, but how his mother had got the better of them 'and thirty quid down.' But the story became so complicated that I could not get it straight. He was related to half the neighbourhood; every street, almost every third house, contained at least one 'auntie' or niece. He said that when his grandmother had died, he and all the other grandchildren had

86

gone to school in mourning. When the teacher, somewhat aghast at seeing half the school in black, asked what had happened, there was a general chorus of 'our grannie's dead, teacher.'

The bombs of the last war were still vivid in his mind; there had been no shelters and there had been panic; screaming women had rushed in all directions in the overcrowded market street, stalls were overturned, and it was easy to pick up a good dinner. On one of these occasions Archie's mother and a crowd of other women had forced their way into the cellars of a brewery for safety, and a Hogarthian orgy ensued. The manager tried to remove them, without success. Angry husbands appeared to drag them away, but they too succumbed to the festive atmosphere. 'Them was good days,' said Archie with a loud sigh. 'We nippers fought we was rich wiv' a 'alfpenny, and look at the prices now—it's wicked.'

Archie lived in a room by himself and shared a sink with two other families, over which there were constant and violent rows, each side accusing the other of disgusting habits. He was very economical, too economical ever to have married; and the moment he got home changed into incredibly disreputable clothes to save his others, although he was not really poor. His economies, in fact, amounted to stinginess. When, one afternoon, he won £60 racing he gave Tommy and Bill 1s. between them, because they were present when he got the good news and he virtually had to, but nobody else saw any of it: and when Admiral Evans treated us all to some beer after a parade, Archie stoutly opposed pooling it and holding a party. He did not drink and he did not smoke; his only extravagance was a weakness for the ladies. The local lady was Jeanie and she charged 8d. Archie took great care to be regular and punctual for Jeanie. We all said that if the area was much more heavily bombed there would be no doorways left, and we should have to build a portable one. However, it did not depend on the bombing; poor Jeanie grew thinner and thinner and finally, I believe, moved off to Hoxton.

Archie was certainly no Adonis; his lower lip and jaw protruded well beyond the upper; he had a purple and blue complexion, and heavy drooping eyelids, over bulging, very white, eyeballs. But he was never daunted, and would make approaches to the most unlikely people. He also had a reprehensible habit of going into surface shelters and switching his torch on suddenly. Surface shelters were never used for proper sheltering, and he would reappear saying, 'Lovely pair of limbs, Barbara, lovely pair of limbs.' During blitzes he was not perhaps at his most useful, but he was a terror for lights. Not a glimmer or a chink escaped him, and he even came in one night saying that the man in the chemist's shop up the road was a fifth columnist, because he was standing in the doorway in a white coat, when a plane was overhead.

He was a peaceful man and would sit in a corner of the hut for hours, silent except for his cough. It was a bad cough, but he never spat indoors. At Post 2 there had been a warden who, despite repeated protests, would hit the stove with a sizzle, but Archie always went outside. It was a good intention, although as the walls were only matchboarding it made no difference to the sound effect. One wet evening, after bringing up his lungs so richly that all of our stomachs heaved, he announced as he came back, '. . . er um . . . it's spitting a little outside,' and was shocked when we laughed. It was not done to mention such things.

At 11.15 Archie made the tea—it was a ritual. Punctually he would fill the electric kettle from the bucket of drinking water and then, provided that the kettle worked, would sit down and gaze distantly at a point a foot above the floor, until it boiled. Once the precious brew was made the teapot was shrouded in a flimsy dish-cloth, and none of us was allowed any until it had 'drawn' for a full fifteen minutes. I was heavily snubbed one night when I said that I rather fancied a slightly paler drink. When all the mugs had been filled, Archie unwrapped his supper. Unless he had been unlucky, it was always the same. Every three days he bought half a knacker (sheep's head) and each evening had a slice sandwiched between two enormous pieces of bread. He ate slowly and noisily, and with great concentration.

Izzie (his real name was William Paleck, but he was always called Izzie because he did not like it) was one of those pathetic figures who ask to be trodden on. One couldn't blame the others. In spite of strong school traditions, I found it a great temptation to tread on him myself. He had good intentions, but deplorable technique. With surprising ingenuousness, he told me one night that he was nervous of crossing the burial grounds after dark. I replied that that was nonsense, and that it was really the safest place, as there were no towering buildings to fall on one. But Izzie was referring to more spectral objects than high explosive bombs. A month later, before he left for the army, I had to eat my words—just as I reached the entrance gates, three HE's crashed into the cemetery, and tombstones hurtled through the air while I lay flat in the gutter. An early Victorian tombstone, I decided, could be as crushing as any other sort of masonry.

Arthur Purton looked like a *Punch* cartoon of a burglar. As far as I know, he was; but only in a small way Occasionally he had a nasty temper but, on the whole, was pleasant enough. His working companion and 'pal,' Stan, was younger and more cheerful; he was very prone to fighting, but unluckily for himself was not very skilled at it. Soon after I went to '13,' he lost all his front teeth in a fight near a shelter; this time the 'other chap' went to hospital for three weeks, having 'slipped in the black-out crossing the road'! We could seldom discover what the various fights were about, but if there was any likelihood of repercussions George Harding entered in the log-book 'an altercation then ensued.' Stan noticed that I was 'always reading a different book' and once kindly replenished my supply with a pile of the most execrable 2d. 'dreadfuls,' of a type that I thought had disappeared even from Farringdon Road market fifteen years earlier.

He seemed to have no nerves—possibly, it was lack of imagination —but the heaviest bombing did not deter him in the least. He always carried the ridiculously inadequate official hatchet, and sometimes acquired 'perquisites' if the raid was bad and noisy. He had a dent in his tin hat which he insisted had been caused by a piece of shrapnel six inches by eight. A piece of that size could hardly fail to break one's neck, but it was never wise to dispute people's bomb stories. At the same time, a number of tin hats did get hit by their owners with hammers in the early days.

Then there was Frank Pilley—'gloomy Frank.' He looked, and was, gloomy. Only once did I hear him make a joke, and then the victim took offence and there was very nearly a fight; so that the wretched Frank announced sulkily, 'I'll never make another joke.' He and George Harding were the only trade unionists, but there was no similarity between them. George considered that trade unions existed to champion his and other workers' rights with vigour, and admitted that many of the big union officials were as remote from such a conception as the employers: he had little use for talking shops. Frank regarded the unions and the Labour Party as many people regard the Bible—not to be questioned, to be taken out and dusted once or twice a year, but never read; certainly no action should ever be taken on its precepts. He refused to join the Civil Defence branch, on the grounds that one union was enough for one man, even when it could no longer help him. At heart he was glad that he now had an excuse for doing nothing. He was secretary of a branch of a small craft union, and he showed me his minute books with great pride; they were a painstaking record of inactivity, drearily written in indelible pencil in a large, pointed handwriting But they were as dear to him as his wife and child.

One night when it was clear there was going to be a fairly heavy raid—two bombs had already dropped within half a mile of us—Frank said he thought he'd 'just pop home and see his books safe.' We thought his anxiety was somewhat overdone, but he insisted on going off to stow his precious minute books in the basement. While he was taking the treasure to safety he met a number of the occupants of his block, and told them that in his opinion it was going to be a heavy night, and they had better go to the shelter. Half an hour later the block was hit; so Frank's dreary records probably saved at least five lives. If his branch never does anything else, it will at least have these five lives to its credit.

He was surly and had a perpetual grievance, but never wanted to do anything about it. His surliness was probably due to his constant conviction that all the world wanted to take advantage of him. Largely from stupidity, and without meaning to do so, he managed to antagonise everybody. He admired Harding, and would take any amount of snubbing from him, so that it was often embarrassing. He resented my presence strongly, as, for one reason, he had no use for women, except as cooks or cleaners, let alone 'my sort.' Fortunately for our spirits, he was away sick for most of the heavy spring raids, as he had a weak chest. I did not see him 'in action' till the final blitz, and then he was more capable than I had imagined he would be, though muddle-headed.

Frank could not abide Arthur Purton; he disapproved of his way of life, and had once had an ugly row with him. He said he was determined to 'shop' him, and tried hard to catch Arthur in pubs, or fire-watching illicitly for some firm, during raids. Arthur, of course, did both of these things, but had too many pals who would tip him off, to get caught. On the night of May 10th Arthur got hit: he had been hit in the leg once before by an incendiary, but this time he got a piece in the neck. He had been in, or at the door of a pub, when an HE came down close by, and a splinter caught him. The publican telephoned the Post and I took the call. As I was giving the address of the pub for the ambulance, Frank came in, and his eyes gleamed— now he had got him. I told him that he was wrong, that Arthur had been in Herald Street and he had only been taken into the pub for shelter. Frank, naturally, knew that I was lying, and it was for him that night to make out the report on CD casualties. I thought Arthur's number was up. In the morning Frank came up to me sheepishly, and said, 'I did make a report on Arthur—er—I said he was—er—hurt while bringing a report to the Post. D'you think that'll be all right?' When Frank was absent we were sorry for him, but within half an hour of his return his surliness and stupidity would infuriate us again.

There were three others on the night shift, a hefty stoker of well over six feet, who was called Tiny, and a young chap—Billy Barker— who had been invalided out of the army, and practised on a trombone in his spare time. Lastly there was George Black, or Georgie 2. He was a charming person—an irrepressible little Cockney, and neither the grossest injustice, nor the most alarming raid, could damp his spirits for very long. He told me, afterwards, that he was always extremely nervous when a raid started, and liked to go away by himself for half an hour; after that he felt better. In any case, it never showed, and by the time that he joined us, and he always did whether he was on duty or 'off,' he was as cheerful as ever.

He was sociable by nature and, apart from George Harding, was the only member of the Post who made any effort at first to make me feel at home. I was very grateful, but found that I could hardly understand a word he said. He was a specialist in rhyming slang, and where tradition had not given him a rhyme, his own delightful fancy would invent one. I knew 'tea-leaf' for thief, 'salmon and trout' for gout, 'plates of meat' for feet, and other simple and basic phrases, but it required great concentration to translate quickly 'elephant's trunk' into drunk, 'Lord Lovell'—shovel, 'Burton-on-Trent'—rent, 'Cain and Able'—table, 'Long Acre'—baker; 'Jenny Lee' might be either tea or flea. In fact, it seemed to me, at first, that it was only Georgie's prepositions that were in normal English.

Rhyming slang is a curious tradition, and still prevalent. Some phrases are used out of a sense of delicacy, others originated as a means of baffling slow-witted policemen, informers, or other similarly noxious listeners. But, for the most part, it is due to a simple delight in jingles and rhymes, and is at the same time a proof of quick-wittedness. It cannot be learnt like other languages. Custom and oral tradition have established the basic rhymes, and a number of other euphemisms. 'Looking as if you hadn't the right change' does not mean puzzled or resentful, but very angry. When Arthur was hit I was told that he 'had got it where Maggie wears the beads' and was uncertain for a moment where exactly that might be.

Georgie was small and wiry and tough. As a kid, he had had very poor health; he was the youngest of a large family, and lost his first two jobs through falling sick. After that he determined to make himself strong, so took a job as a packer, and insisted on carrying large crates on his head for a half-mile journey, instead of using a barrow. The cure worked more effectively than the 'keep fit' exercises and vibrant massage practised in Hampstead, and the West End. He was fond of drawing female nudes and decorated the Post with them; he liked music, 'it was the only good thing about religion,' and was a very good dart player.

Soon after I had moved to '13' I learnt a new word, a word which became the basic expression of our vocabularies for the next two years. One night, when there was heavy gunfire and a large number of planes about, Stan came in to tell us that he had 'poodled in home, to find the old woman in bed—I didn't arf ruck 'er.' Rucking means a more vociferous and energetic form of grumbling—one can have a ruck, or be a good rucker. We were quite good ruckers at '13,' we rucked about the free bath tickets after heavy raids, and we rucked about our food vouchers when we found we were being diddled out of 6d. From the Town Hall's point of view, anyone who could speak his mind twice in the same vein was a rucker.

When there was no raid we usually played darts to fill in the time; sometimes it was cards, but the pack was so well worn that Arthur and Stan could recognise their opponents' hands. Occasionally we had a conversation, but there was not a very wide selection of subjects. Racing and boxing were the most frequent topics, but the war, religion, anti-Semitism and similar debatable subjects did occasionally get their share of time. Religion did not last long as, for once in our discussions, there was too much unanimity.

'Religion's all right for the ones that runs it.'

'They make a packet out of it.'

' 'Course some parsons is OK.'

'How many?'

'Look at that bloke at St. Simon's. When we asked him if the kids in the shelter below could use his large room for games with the nurses—no—not unless they came to his church first.'

'The only thing you can say for it, is the music. I got into Westminster once, and the singing was lovely.'

'Oh, it's a lot of baloney—— 'Course I always see my kids go to Sunday school. Gets 'em out of the way. I didn't 'alf wallop our Bert last Sunday for dodgin'.'

Anti-Semitism proved more controversial; we were on the borders of a Jewish quarter, where Mosley had made a propaganda drive before the war. Nevertheless, as is usual, most of the stories against the Jews were second-hand.

'Yids stink.'

'Not all Yids. There's good and bad.'

'I worked for a Yid once—no complaints.'

'Yus—an' I worked for one who'd sweat the skin off his own family.'

'They stick together too much.'

'You can't blame them for that; no one else would do it for them.'

'The Black Market's all Yids.'

'No, it isn't. The papers make more of a song about it when it's a Yid that gets caught.'

'Did you hear about that doctor needlin' a bloke with sugar to give him dia——whatever it is, to dodge the call up? He was a Yid.'

'They're in all the easy money—pictures, food, and all that lark. All the big concerns, you find Yids at the top.'

'But if the Yids didn't get in there, the others would—we'd be no better off.'

'All the rich are the same—Yids or not.'

'Well, yes.'

'Sammy Harmon's a Yid—he's all right.'

'Oh yes, *he's* all right.'

'And Joe and Hymie.'

'Oh yes, they're all right; there's Yids and Yids.'

'This anti-Yid business is a racket—always find another bloke to take the rap.'

'Anyway, what do you want to do about them? Exterminate them, like Hitler?'

'Oh no. But I'll lay you, a lot of them Jews only minded Hitler 'cause he turned on *them*.'

'Yes, the rich ones. But there's no sense in blaming the Jews for everything; in Liverpool they put it all on the Irish, but it doesn't get *us* anywhere.'

'The Irish stink.'

'Oh gawd, who does smell nice?'

'Yids won't do a day's work.'

'They work damn hard sometimes.'

'Yus, at their own business.'

'Don't come it, Stan, no one's ever seen you do much of a day's work '

7

January-March

WHEN the siren went, those who were not already on their sectors (the Post was divided into seven sectors) went off to them. That left three at the Post as a rule—the Post Warden, his deputy and myself, and the two who were responsible for the adjoining sectors, within call, if not actually at the Post. I was never given a specific sector, and became a species of General Purpose Warden. When planes were coming overhead we all trooped out into the street. Our wooden hut had already been blown in and burnt twice, and no one fancied sitting inside it. It was bitterly cold. The Post was at a crossroads, and the wind rushed at you from all directions. There was a concrete pill-box under the hut, which was certainly safe, but four people in it made a crowd, and it was damp and had only a microscopic electric fire. Most important, it was almost impossible to judge the direction of any sounds when you were down there, as the staircase turned round twice in its descent. So, for the most part, we stood in the street and stamped our feet. I had been given a leather coat for Christmas, and an Orkney Island seaman's jersey of immense proportions. I wore an old pair of pyjamas under my trousers, and acquired two pairs of golf stockings from my father-in-law, and the only 'comfort' I ever received—a four-foot knitted scarf from the WVS. I wore all of this and had a mountainous appearance, but I was still cold. Warm uniforms and overcoats were not issued to wardens until five months after the blitzes had ceased.

Periodically, George Harding and I went off on a tour of the district. We looked up the other wardens, and visited the shelters. The latter were always full, but we seldom had any trouble in them. Bunks had recently been installed in most, and only in exceptional circumstances did they suffer from damp. The chief shelter marshal of the area had been well known in the district since he was a baby, and was still called Bobsie, although he was over sixty. He had called himself by that name as a child and it had stuck. He was a Councillor and the only one I met who could really be called a socialist, and who, disinterestedly, considered that it was part of his job to look after the citizens whom he represented. There may have been others, but I did not meet them. He kept a little shop up the street, and he knew everyone and all their troubles. He advised them where to get relief and followed the case up, and saw that they got it. He would interview recalcitrant husbands, and soothe anxious parents who thought that the courting of the adolescents was becoming too realistic. At first he had allowed card-playing in his shelters, but one Friday night he found that a boy of sixteen had lost his entire week's wages and had nothing to hand over to his mother. Bobsie lent him the money, but there was never any more card-playing.

Our borough gained a reputation for gambling in shelters, but that was not till after the blitzes. When the shelters were full, there were enough responsible citizens and shelter marshals to control it. But later, when they were only half-full, and the more uncomfortable ones were quite empty, the practice grew rapidly. The local tough boys made a regular habit of it and constantly fleeced the less 'wide.' It was as common with children under fourteen. I have even seen a child of less than two, and still in nappies, dicing for half-pennies with girls of eight and nine, and boys of twelve. It was not easy to check. You couldn't ignore it; but if you stopped them they only moved into the lavatories and continued there, which was unhygienic into the bargain; and if you turned them out of the shelter they got into worse trouble in the back alleys.

Later, also, juvenile 'swiping' was very extensive. It was so easy. Even when the piles of damaged furniture and other property in the streets had been at last removed, most houses and warehouses had suffered from blast and were easy of entry. I once arranged for a batch of children under twelve from a very poor street to go to the Zoo. The next night, to show their gratitude, they asked me if I would like some bulbs. Uncertain whether they meant daffodils or electric ones, I rightly assumed the latter. 'We'd let you 'ave a dozen for two bob, miss.' I asked where they had got them, and suggested a firm further down the street. 'Yes, miss, it's easy, miss, when the fire-watchers goes to the pub. Won't you 'ave 'em, miss, dozen for tenpence?'

Some of them were better business men than this story implies, with its rapid reduction in price. There was little Pozzie, aged eleven, who could pipe a rather smutty song about Hitler with great success. He had ten baby rabbits which he wanted to sell for 10s. He well knew that at that age he was not allowed to trade, and with much circumlocution, therefore, entered into negotiations with a coster. ' 'E wasn't 'alf tight, miss, 'e'd only give me nine bob. I told 'im I must 'ave ten, but no, 'e wouldn't. So I let 'em go for nine, but when 'e wasn't lookin', I sneaked one of 'em back, and sold it round the corner for a bob.'

In one of the shelters where, later, play centres were organised, all the equipment disappeared three times. It was puzzling, as the shelter was locked all day and all night, except when the centre was in progress. No one slept in it, as part had been flooded when the building above was burnt out. But clearly, there must be some alternative means of entry, and one afternoon I and two wardens determined not to give up until we found it. We looked everywhere and got filthy. We climbed through a hole in the ceiling and got into the remains of the premises overhead; we squeezed through windows and up twisted fire escapes, but it only led us to the roof of the next firm, and not even the drainpipes provided a way in.

After two and a half hours we found it. In the furthest cubicle of the lavatory bay there was a twelve-inch gap between the wall and the ceiling. In the ordinary way it was too dark there for it to be noticed, but if you crawled through that you dropped down into a completely disused and separate bay, which for some inexplicable reason had been bricked off and forgotten. It had an emergency exit into an alley-way, which could barely be seen from the outside. Here, we found an amazing assortment of goods; very few of the toys, but fifty cases each containing 500 metal boxes stolen from the firm next door, a gas cooking stove, a billiard table lamp, sets of 'housey-housey,' blankets, saucepans, a chopper, and iron bars. Unfortunately we were seen climbing out, and though we were certain that a lad called Snorty was one of the gang leaders, we could not prove it as the hide-out was never used again.

Before going back to the Post, if it was not yet 10.30 p.m., George and I called in at Bill and Con's, as the 'Cross Keys' was called, for a pint. Most of the pubs in the district closed down as soon as the siren went. At the first sound of the 'wobbler,' 'Time, gentlemen, please,' was called, and you had to go. But unless the raid was exceptionally heavy, Bill and Con stayed open. Bill and Con's was a friendly pub. They, and the customers, who were mostly railway or factory workers or street traders, quickly accepted me, although I was a 'foreigner' living in a remote area a mile and a half away, and I could always go in and have a chat or a game of darts. There was also—to my delight—a ladies' lavatory.

Our telephone exchange had been burnt out in the City fire, and for three months we had no telephone at the Post. This had one great advantage; we were blissfully free of interference from the Town Hall. We were too far away to get many visitors, and since we were not on the phone, we were left alone. But as the first job of a warden is to report casualties and damage as quickly as possible, it was a scandalously long time to leave the Post unconnected. Private firms nearby got a line again long before we did. Every time that a bomb fell, we had to go three-quarters of a mile to the next Post to send a report. It added unnecessary risks, and increased our inefficiency. The neglect also added to our general impression that the authorities were not much concerned with our well-being. The police box had had its phone re-connected almost immediately after the fire. Our difficulties were added to by the fact that the Post was situated at the extreme easterly end of the area, and when George was that side he could never be sure whether the wardens on the other side had already reported a bomb or not.

" Classical music."

One Tuesday night, within ten minutes of the 'wobbler,' a heavy one came down on Liverpool Street station. This was just off our 'beat,' about five minutes' walk away, but Stan disappeared unostentatiously. He was an inveterate hanger-on of bomb damage, and would rush off to incidents that were no concern of ours. It was not until he had left to go into the army that I found out why. He would certainly not have taken anything from a private dwelling, but about a business firm he had not the same scruples. It left us short-handed, and already there was a constant stream of planes overhead. Suddenly there was a rending rushing sound, someone said 'This is ours—jump!' But before he had said it, all four of us had leapt higgledy-piggledy down the narrow steps to the pill-box. It landed on a tobacco firm thirty yards up the street, and brought the front crashing down into the road. There were, as a rule, seven or eight shelterers in the basement and three or four fire-watchers.

Harding turned to me and said: 'Hop on your bike, Barbara, and send an "Express" from Post 12.' For an instant I had the unreasonable thought 'Why pick on me?', but it was clearly unreasonable, as I was easily the youngest and quickest of the four there. I got on my bike and pedalled hard. The next day I could not make out why I was so stiff in the arms, until it dawned on me that I had unconsciously gripped the handle-bars as though I was hanging on for my life. Another plane seemed to be following me along the main road. It was like a Walt Disney film. When I turned to the left at a crossroads, the plane seemed to turn to the left also. The machine seemed to have eyes of its own glued on me only, out of all the nine million Londoners. Like Mickey, I too whistled, to pretend to myself that I was unconcerned. Its engine staggered and rose, and, abruptly, I stopped whistling. The load came down, one to my right and one ahead. Both were more than a hundred yards away, but I felt it was really too much, and got off my bike to think about it. In earlier raids I had been on foot, and generally had had company: I felt much more insecure on a bicycle, and very lonely and microscopic by myself, in the middle of a nightmare London. However, any danger there had been was over, and I went on and sent the report, adding that, as I came along, something had dropped on their area nearby and that their wardens would probably soon be in with the news.

As I left there was a cheering chorus of 'Mind how you go.' I assured them that my mother had always told me to be particularly careful where I went after dark, and rode off. A set of flares was coming down, and it rapidly grew so light that, in an access of economy, I switched off my bicycle lamp. They were shooting at the flares, or their parachutes, and a fragment of something hit my tin hat with a ping. I began to feel a bit of a hero. When I got back, Harding said that they had got the eight people out easily; they were only a bit dusted up. 'Go back and send the MI Report through, will you?' My budding feeling of heroism immediately disappeared like smoke. This time I passed a good-sized fire on my right, and ahead both sides of the road were blazing fiercely, but fire appliances were already clanging along to deal with them.

As I returned for the second time, Harding was walking up the street, over the débris, with a couple of policemen. I called after him that I would catch them up, and went down the steps to the pill-box to fetch my eye-shield, as the dust and dirt in the air were still thick. At that moment another HE came rushing down. I started up the steps and promptly got blown down again. When I reached the top I saw that the bomb had fallen on almost exactly the same spot as the previous one, only this time in the middle of the road, and just where I had last seen Harding. I did not see how he could have missed it. I shouted to the others, and ran up the street, dreading the bits and pieces that I was certain would be all that I would find of him, and scrambling clumsily and recklessly over the pile of débris. I trod on the corner of a piece of corrugated iron, which sprang up and hit me on the nose. The dust was so thick that you could not keep your eyes open, and when you shouted it seemed to fill your mouth and blanket the sound.

I mustered all my breath, and gave a final yell of 'George!' If he didn't answer that, he wouldn't answer anything; it would mean digging, and the others had not followed me. I was rewarded with a 'Coming.' He now thought that it was I that was hurt. We joined forces in the middle of the scrapheap, and expressed our great pleasure at meeting again. Two seconds before the bomb had struck, he had turned into a large granite doorway. He had not heard it coming down, and had felt the earth give before the sound of the explosion practically deafened him. I said, 'It's nice to see you.' 'Yes,' he answered, 'bit of luck.' At this point we became conscious of a mighty roaring and bellowing from the roof. It was one of the fire-watchers, a lad from Norfolk, but Harding decided that he could not make all that noise if he were really hurt. We learnt later that he had been on the roof when the thing hurtled past him, and had jumped to the conclusion that the front staircase must have been blown away and so had tried the fire-escape. Unfortunately for him, this had—it ended in mid-air. While he was climbing back again, and groping through the building, an ammonia plant got turned on, and he decided that the end of the world had come.

A gas main was burning in the crater in the road, but, to my delight, another fire-watcher told us that the telephone in his building was working, which meant that I should not have to bicycle to '12' again. There was a strong shelter down below, so well reinforced with concrete, and with steel doors, that they had hardly even felt any vibration, although the explosion had been almost overhead. We went down two flights of stairs to telephone. I had not yet given my appearance a thought, but I was well coated with the dust of two bombs, and my energetic cycling had made the sweat trickle down, leaving paler zig-zags of face to show through. This gave me an entirely spurious reputation for some weeks of being 'that brive girl wiv' the dirty fice,' and we could be certain of being treated in any of the local houses—in any, that is, except the 'Duke of York's.'

At the 'Duke of York's' we had been unfortunate. Archie had seen an incendiary bomb hit the roof, so George and Tiny had gone to investigate. The landlord had not been very interested when they told him, but said they could go up and have a look if they liked. They found it wedged in a chimney. They tried to lever it out, but it was stuck fast, so they poured buckets of water and sand down. When finally it was extinguished they went downstairs, feeling proud of themselves, and confident of at least a pint each, to be met by an irate landlord with a sooty face, and a knot of angry customers looking like black and white minstrels. Soot was everywhere—on the counter, on the chairs, and in the beer. George and Tiny beat a hasty retreat.

When we got back to the Post, the other George arrived breathlessly, having heard that a bomb had dropped almost on it. We were all three so pleased to see each other that we enjoyed the rest of the night. We did not have much more trouble, but we did not mind anyway.

The gas main continued to burn brightly. We were not allowed to tamper with them, so we stood on the corner of the street thirty yards away. Occasionally people passed us, hurrying to a shelter. They all stopped and helpfully pointed out the fire to us. We said 'Yes, we know,' and they said 'Oh,' and went more hurriedly on. Then a drunk came up and told us we were a lot of mucking b——s not to put the fire out: we were thieves, cowards and scroungers, and he'd show us. George started to take off his coat, and the man retreated to the middle of the road, shouting elaborate abuse at us, until a trolley bus all but ran over him. Periodically, a gas company van arrived, the men would get out, look wisely at the fire, find that they had not got the right tools, and drive away again. The flames were about eight foot high, and although there was nothing for them to catch, we thought that they were quite sufficient to attract another bomb. One gang went so far as to open up a manhole nearby, but they said that they could not find the connection, and they too went away. Just after the all-clear had sounded, a man drove up, wedged a plug in the broken end, and the fire was out!

We had had no hospital casualties, and the two Georges and myself had become firm friends. It was a good night. I realised that I was extremely glad that I had come to '13.'

Before Christmas 1940 the raids had been continuous. Almost every night enemy aircraft had been over London in considerable numbers, and even when there was an all-clear about midnight, another alert would follow within half an hour or an hour. But they were not widespread blitzes: scattered areas would 'get a packet,' one, one night—another, the next. Occasionally there would be a large-scale disaster, as when, by ill-luck, a bomb would hit the lift shaft, or other weak spot, of a tube station and crash right down to the crowded platform and passages below. Moonlit nights had not been much more fearsome than the dark ones: the tonnage dropped on us was only slightly heavier, and was offset by the increased visibility.

But after January 1941, the full moon came to be dreaded by all of us, and with good reason. Each time that the moon was at the full, the raids were heavier than anything London had yet experienced, with the exception of the docks on the first week-end. The attacks of March 14th-15th surpassed those of February; April surpassed those of March; and May eclipsed them all.

On one of the March raids the Café de Paris was hit. The melodramatic nature of the incident caught the fancy of the reporters, and for three days the papers were full of the gallantries of expensive girls who had torn their expensive dance frocks into strips to make bandages. The reporters seemed surprised; but the most light-headed society girl would not refuse a strip of her skirt in such circumstances. Even forty guineas cannot weigh against another's life-blood. It was a gory incident, but the same week another dance-hall a mile to the east of us was hit and there were nearly two hundred casualties. This time there were only 10s. 6d. frocks, and a few lines in the paper followed by, 'It is feared there were several casualties.' Local feeling was rather bitter. At the end of the week one or two papers which had actually implied that it was a com-mendable thing to go to the Café de Paris, for instance, and thereby show that the air-blitz was not affecting West End morale, now said that to go to a local 'hop' was irresponsible and flippant.

Again, when a substantial section of Oxford Street was burned it was front-page news, although there were so few casualties. We could lose two blocks of flats, and many small shops which were the sole means of livelihood of their owners, and there would only be a terse notice, saying 'Bombs were dropped in —— district; there were a few casualties.' Visitors from the country, wearing the stricken expressions of mourners in the third carriage of a funeral procession, would say, 'Have you seen Lewis's? Isn't it terrible?' But what did the loss of these big stores mean? So much stock of women's clothing gone up in smoke, so many shares not being paid, so many assistants who would be out of work for a short time, or who could go into the Services. They were insured, they generally had branches and stores of stock in the country. We felt that old Mrs. Hick's stocking-full of her life's savings, even if it only amounted to £20, was of more real value. Neither could we see that the death of Lord —— and his family, who were killed by an unlucky bomb on their country residence, was any more important than that of Bill Hardman, who was killed at his job on the railway two nights after all his family, except one little girl who had been evacuated to the country, had been crushed and drowned.

Reporters did not come down our way unless we provided a grand spectacle like the City fire. Our people did not mind not being in the news, but the excessive publicity given to the rich and their haunts was, to say the least, tactless. The emphasis given to the importance

Overleaf: John Lewis's in Oxford Street and the local shop suffered the same fate, but did not necessarily receive the same attention from the authorities

of their troubles inevitably created the impression that ours were of less significance. Equally, the Government emphasis on the saving of property, though no doubt necessary, had an unfortunate effect. Surely, business firms could be compelled to employ fire-watchers without the implication that their stocks were more important than life. When it was ever a case of Mrs. Hick's stocking and her iron bed and chest of drawers *or* a business firm, none of us, and none of the firemen, hesitated. Mrs. Hicks had it.

Some of the older women, with that traditional humility of the poor that social workers like to find, would shake their heads mournfully and clack their tongues over Lord and Lady —— and 'the poor ladies in that café,' but the younger ones and the men were growing bitter, and would silence them with 'What about us?' Then there would be a scornful chorus of 'Nobody cares about us. We don't matter.' 'We're the Front Line, we are.' 'I wouldn't mind being the Front Line if there was any other bleeding lines.' 'This ain't no war. My Bert's been polishin' buttons and scrubbin' floors ever since January last.' And the inevitable ending, 'Oh well, it's the first ten years that's the hardest.'

The war was not going well, and was discussed more than it had been since its declaration. During March and April we won in Ethiopia, but lost in Libya; we went into Greece and we came out again; the Greeks were forced to surrender; Jugoslavia 'found its soul,' and lost its independence. At the Post, gloomy Frank would often start the conversation with his refrain:

'It's just the same as the last war.'

'Gawd! You always say that. It's not the same. This is supposed to be a war against the Fascists.'

'It's the same. It won't do *us* any good.'

'But if the Nazis won you'd have Mosley, and Ramsey, and their thugs in the Government.'

'You wouldn't be secretary of your little trade union branch then, Frank.'

'Oh, you won't ever get Fascism here '

'Why not—if we lost?'

'We won't lose.'

'Well, I don't see as we're winning much.'

'It'll go on for a bit more, then they'll fix it. There'll be an agreement or something—settle it all.'

The end of Fuller's Restaurant and business as usual for an East End seamstress

'You can't have agreements with Fascism, without going Fascist yourself.'

'Oh, it'll be all right—you see.'

'All we've done all right is evacuations.'

'It's the high-ups as don't seem keen on this war.'

'Churchill is.'

'Oh yes—*he* is.'

'What this Government wanted is a war against Russia.'

'They'll have it, when they want it. You see.'

'Stalin wants to keep out of the war.'

'Who wouldn't?'

'He won't be able to.'

'He's a damn sight cleverer than old Chamberlain.'

'Everyone wants a smack at Russia.'

'Well I don't. I'm not a b—— Communist, but I think there's a lot of things not so bad there. I think the ordinary chap there gets a better deal than we do—many ways.'

'It's the same as the last war. Last time it was the Kaiser, this time it's Hitler.'

'The Kaiser and Hitler aren't the same. There was only one Kaiser, but you've got Hitlers in this country too, same as in France.'

'France was rotten.'

'And everything in the garden here is lovely.'

'Supposing Germans was marching up Regent Street. What would you do?'

'They'll never do that. They'll fix something.'

'What's the good of fixing anything—no more than "fixing" a cat.'

'You may know a lot, but I was in the last war—and it's just the same—except for the bombing.'

'Anyway, what can we do about it?'

'Oh, it's the first ten years. . . .'

'There was a hundred years' war, once.'

And so on, and so on.

Except for the fools, who blankly asserted that it would all be all right in the end, because they did not want to think at all, Londoners were perplexed. But they went on enduring the raids with a grumbling fortitude that in many ways was heroic. Since they had not in any way been prepared for the horrors of bombing, this dogged endurance was all the more impressive.

8

Full Moon and Fires

APRIL 16th. The siren blew at 9 p.m. Before we had put on our coats and tin hats there was a steady drone of aircraft overhead. When we got into the street the whole sky seemed to be full of aeroplanes, the air itself was throbbing with their engines. Harding said '. . . um—sounds as though it's going to be good.' He was correct. The newspapers next morning said that Hitler had used 450 aeroplanes, and many of those had made a double or triple journey. For the next six hours there was hardly a moment when an enemy plane was not within earshot; as soon as the sound of one faded away to the north, another followed it in from the south. The gunfire was heavy, and when that stopped for a time we could occasionally hear the whine of a night-fighter. We were glad enough to hear them; and we learnt later that they had brought down thirty-two, but at the time they seemed to make no difference at all to the steady, exasperating drone that continued throughout the night.

For the first half-hour we stood in the street listening to bombs whistling down on neighbouring districts. We all grew extremely apprehensive. The beginning of a raid, before there is anything to do locally, is by far the worst part of it. Your imagination leaps ahead of even the most gory 'incident,' and you have sickening doubts about your possible behaviour. Once there is something to do, this self-consciousness disappears.

Suddenly, the street and the buildings lit up. We looked up, and saw three chandelier flares descending slowly, directly above us. Two gave off the usual reddish amber light, the third was greenish. Three at once would be too many for the gunners to hit before the next plane came in. The light grew brighter and brighter. Tiny, who had a long gaunt face, looked like an El Greco painting. No one made any comments, and I felt very cold. One was rooted to the spot, as in a nightmare when one's legs refuse to move. The light

grew so bright that it paled the full moon; it shone eerily through the empty windows of the buildings opposite, and gleamed green on the charred walls and twisted girders. All I could think of was Lewis Carroll's nonsense rhyme:

> ' 'Twas brillig and the slithy toves
> Did gyre and gimble in the wabe.'

Ordinary words would not fit such a weirdly dismal scene.

Streams of tracer bullets were rising slowly and gracefully towards the flares, and suddenly two of them went out. Someone sighed—probably myself—but at that moment the next plane came in. It dropped its load when it was almost overhead, and as a bomb crashed nearby, George said that that should be one of ours, and we went off to see. Guided by the cloud of dust that rose a second or two later, we found it, but it was just the other side of our boundary and the wardens of that borough arrived as soon as we did, so we wished them joy and came back.

We sat in the pill-box for a bit, but neither of us had anything to say. Our state of tension was suddenly broken by a load of incendiaries, and we rushed around with sand-bags and buckets, very glad to have something to do. As soon as we had got them out, another

The blazing fires of St Paul's Churchyard

load clattered down further up the road, then a third. Most fell in the open and were easily covered. George came out of the front garden of a Welsh chapel saying that he had put half a dozen daffodils on one, as he couldn't waste a sand-bag. The pastor was particularly proud of his daffodils, and we laughed gaily at the thought of his Welsh indignation.

In the next side street we found that a deserted pub was alight. It was exactly the right-sized fire for a stirrup pump, and sufficiently large to give one a sense of pride in not having to call the Fire Brigade. So I trotted off to the Post, picked up a pump, and struggled back with two full buckets. I was looking forward to some stirrup-pump exercise, and was devising means by which I could get the nozzle and leave George the hard work of pumping; but when I got there, there was no George, and I couldn't even distinguish which had been the pub. An oil bomb had come down in my absence and the whole block on that side of the street was blazing. It would need at least three fire appliances, and, as the Brigade drove up, I felt extremely foolish with my ridiculously inadequate gear, and hid it in a doorway.

A huge cloud of dust was rising to my right. In my zeal to fetch the stirrup pump I had not heard anything particularly close, but an HE must have come down at the same time as the oil bomb, and George had probably gone off to that. Those peculiarly compact clouds were proof enough of HE. When there was a breeze they sailed majestically along above the roof tops, looking solid enough to transport a modern Elijah. However dirty the building had been, its cloud of pulverised atoms looked wonderfully white; this one was turning pink at the edges in the reflected firelight. I never ceased to be astonished at the translation of imposing edifices into these piles of cloud. They seemed more like the work of a djinn in a fairy tale than of a prosaic 500 lb. of TNT in a steel case. I found George inspecting the débris, but the building had already been hit once before, so that the further damage was of no consequence, and we went back to the Post to send through a routine report of that and the fires.

Ten minutes later a stick of four came down and did not explode. Two landed in our 'open spaces,' or devastated area, and could wait till morning. George went off to investigate the third. While he was away another load of incendiaries arrived. At this rate there would

Fighting the incendiary bombs on the rooftops

soon be no sand-bags left. A fire-watcher came to help me. When we had finished I sat down exhausted on the remaining dozen bags.

'Aren't you from Watkins'?' I asked.

'Yes,' he answered, and gave me a cigarette.

'Thanks,' I said, 'I thought you were,' and found a match. 'Look at your lovely roof!'

'Blimey!' he said, and dashed off. It was flickering brightly, with the white light that incendiaries give off before they catch hold, but I was too tired to return the assistance he had given me.

By now an enormous fire was burning on the other side of the river. It looked like half a mile of unbroken flame. We had several fair-sized ones ourselves, and George No. 2 must be having a lively time over on his side. George Harding came back, having found his UXB hole. It was advantageously situated in the middle of the parade ground of the local drill hall, and would absolve the Home Guard from parades for at least a week. Just then long flames shot up from what looked like the brewery, on the other side: as there was a shelter underneath it we thought we had better go over and investigate. It was George 2's ground, but if shelterers had to be moved he would need help. No sooner had we crossed the road towards it than an HE whistled down, and crashed a hundred yards behind us. High explosive causes more casualties than fire, so we turned back.

It had sliced the top floor off a large modern building and landed in the space between two shelters. No one in the shelters was hurt, and the fire-watchers had left the roof five minutes before for their cup of tea, so we started off again for the brewery. Hardly had we gone fifty yards when another HE came down behind us, and for the second time we turned back. Three times we started for that fire, but we did not reach it for another two hours.

Our trombone player, Billy Barker, arrived, running, and said that G Block on the other side had received a direct hit, and nine or ten people were trapped. We phoned an express report through and hurried over there with the incident lamps. Bombs seemed to be whistling down somewhere every two minutes. One plane let eight go on the same place. They pounded down with the regularity of Big Ben chiming; we couldn't see where they were striking, but from the sound they were about half a mile away. We stopped—counting them off on our fingers. At the end George said quietly, 'Gawd, there

The constant battle to keep the flames under control

can't be anything left there.' Wherever it was must have been pulverised completely.

As we went on I experienced the only premonition that I have ever felt. I became suddenly convinced that I should not be there for breakfast. The fact that I had never suffered from such intuitions before only increased my certainty that by the morning I should not exist. Even from a rational point of view it did not seem possible that we could continue to be missed, when there were so many 'objects' dropping all around. Although there was nothing one could do about it, it was a disconcerting feeling. Fortunately, however, during the next half-hour, it was submerged by pressure of other business.

George 2 met us and said that there was no one trapped after all; several people had been in the block when it was hit, but they had managed to get out. An ambulance, with a very smart and efficient-looking driver, arrived, and we told her she was not needed. As we did so, some of the neighbours began to insist that four people *were* there; then someone else contradicted this and said that those four were down a nearby shelter. The ambulance driver said, a little acidly, that she would wait while we made up our minds, and very sensibly went to attend to some minor cuts. But it is not an easy matter to assess casualties or 'missing' in a block of flats. With smaller residential houses it is possible to be fairly certain how many should be there, though even then there may always be a visitor who has been prevented from going home by the raid. But in the case of a block of flats, although the regular die-hards who refuse to go to a shelter are known, a number of people may, at any given moment, have gone back upstairs to boil a kettle, or fetch a blanket, and got caught.

The whole of the end wing had come down. We went in at the nearest negotiable entrance to see if we could settle the controversy. Neither George nor I had brought a torch; the general firelight was so bright that it had seemed a ridiculous encumbrance in the street, but inside the ruined building it was utterly black, and we suffered for our laziness as we groped and stumbled over fallen furniture and walls. We could hear whimpering through one wall, and thought that it was a little boy. But there was no way through, and George kicked and banged, and shouted encouraging nonsense. George 2 joined us with the Heavy Rescue Squad. They could not hope to tunnel through the vast pile of débris outside quickly enough without a

The front line of defence, with the war in the heart of London, and members of the Fire Brigade at greatest risk

crane, and so decided to hack a way through from the inside, where we were. The rest of the block looked gimcrack enough, but that wall withstood all the crowbars and picks of the Heavy Rescue for an hour.

When they did manage to open a small hole, we could see that it was not a boy, but an old man. He was pinned underneath a table, and all the seven stories seemed to be piled on top of that in a solid mass. The MO arrived, but the hole was far too small even for him to get through, though he had a reputation for crawling through the most awkward and unlikely apertures, in order to give casualties a shot of morphia. He appeared at almost every incident with which I was concerned, if there were casualties, and never showed the slightest perturbation.

The Heavy Rescue Squad worked hard; as soon as one man became exhausted, another took his place, but it was four hours before the old fellow was extricated, and in the meanwhile we had to go off to other incidents. At the next one there were two casualties, but they were killed outright, and all that was needed was to cover them till daylight. Periodically, we went back to see how they were getting on with the old man. A little knot of relatives or friends had gathered in the street, apparently unconscious of the droning of planes overhead, which went on with exasperating regularity. When at last the hole was big enough to take a stretcher, they carried him to the ambulance. It was only thirty yards away, but before he reached it he was dead. One felt irrationally annoyed. The fact that he died, despite all the tools and the men's energy, increased our general feeling of impotence. One of the man's relatives shook his fist angrily at the invisible Nazis in the sky, and swore. Ridiculous and ineffectual though the gesture might be, there was no other way of relieving his feelings.

The brewery that we had three times tried to visit was still burning fiercely. The firemen had got there quickly, but the water supply had been spasmodic. Arthur appeared, and told us that the vaults below were still intact, but the beer would be warming up soon. We decided that it was not yet necessary to move the people from the shelter. Fires were everywhere. There was a huge conflagration to the south of us, another almost as big to the north, and we had ten large ones of our own. At this point I produced some chocolate; George found a cigarette, which we divided, and we sat down on a doorstep for a meal. The chocolate tasted fine, but we hadn't got a match. I applied to a fireman. He hadn't got one either. A third of our area was blazing brightly, and we could not get a light.

The lack of telephones in our area was a continual worry. Even when the one at the Post was working, it was at the farthest point from the resident population, who could not afford such luxuries. In between was devastation, often difficult to negotiate. The big firms were, for the most part, gutted or evacuated, and the blocks of flats, and the small shops in the back streets did not many of them possess one. At 2 a.m. we needed an ambulance urgently and were a long way from the Post, so we decided to see if old Bobsie would come out and open his shop for us. We found him in his shelter, chatting to all his protégés. Very few were asleep. They had heard muffled but close explosions all the night, and several times the shelter had rocked and swayed. Bobsie certainly looked somewhat alarmed at the thought of coming out. It requires far more strength of mind to come out into the middle of a heavy raid than to stay in the streets all the time. Nevertheless, he came. When we reached the road, as though especially to greet poor Bobsie, an oil bomb whirred down with a roar. In those days they were clumsily made, and seemed to turn over and over on the way down, making a far more alarming noise than an HE. Bobsie spreadeagled himself in the middle of the street, and while I was still arguing with myself whether the open road, or the lee of the houses, was the safer, the thing landed, and the danger was over. Bobsie was shaking a bit, and had trouble with the lock, so, once inside, he and I discussed the question of food supplies (he was a grocer) while George telephoned. He need not have come out; his job was down the shelter, and he could easily have said that his telephone was out of order. We were very grateful to him.

Another of our blocks of flats was hit. George stopped an excited little man who gave us the information. The back of his jacket had been blown off. The front was still intact, and the sleeves were still there, but when he turned round there was nothing left below his collar, except a jagged frill between the shoulder seams. We wondered whether he knew, or whether he was still too excited to feel the draught.

We had been very lucky as regards casualties, but the repeated trotting from one incident to the next, or to find a telephone, was physically tiring, and the everlasting drone of the planes overhead was becoming unbearable. By 3 a.m. we felt that there was not ever going to be any end to it; it would go on all the next day, and all the next night; it would go on until nothing was left. I had a picture of London after three weeks of non-stop bombing of this intensity—flat, from Victoria to Greenwich. I said: 'Suppose it goes on all day to-morrow, as well as to-morrow night.' George said: 'That's it. Be cheerful!'

The Town-Clerk-cum-Controller came to visit us, and we enquired how the rest of the borough was faring. Apparently our area had had the most concentrated attention, but there had been over sixty incidents already. I asked if Post 2 had had anything, and he said, oh yes, they had had one in the square in which I lived—two houses had had their tops sliced off by an HE. But he was incapable of remembering on which side of the square they had been. I explained why I was anxious, but still he could not remember. My 'old man,' as Post 13 called him, was up in London this night, and all evening it had been an additional anxiety every time a bomb fell in that direction, although he was quite as capable of looking after himself as I was. I wanted to telephone, but dared not, as, whether my home was still standing or not, I should probably get no answer and, therefore, be even more worried. If a bomb had come down so close he would certainly have gone out to try and give a hand.

A UXB had come down nearby and we trudged off in that direction. I was never optimistic of finding them, and also had a sneaking feeling that the day shift would have both a better chance of success, and more peaceable conditions in which to conduct the search. However, this time we came across it almost by accident—a neat round hole in the middle of the road about two-feet-six in diameter. That meant one of the largest sizes in bombs. It was exactly on the dividing line of our Post area and the next. We went to the next Post, and had an argument as to whose hole it was. They said they did not want it; and we felt that we had had enough.

On the way back we met two policemen; compared with us in our dirty, dusty overalls, they looked smart and immaculate, and we asked them to put up a road barrier. They and George peered down the hole, giving it a thorough and lengthy examination. I was frankly nervous, and after some time pointed out that some of these things sometimes went off. They rather laughed at the frightened little woman, but we had not left it long when it exploded and blew a thirty-foot crater. I felt justified.

More oil bombs came down and another large fire shot up two streets away. But it was nearly 4.30 a.m., and the planes were becoming less frequent. I started timing the intervals: five minutes in which there were no aircraft to be heard. We dared to hope that, perhaps, soon it would be over. The glare and smoke of the fires had almost hidden the moon for hours. All night we could have read small newsprint easily by the firelight. But now the sky grew paler and the dawn came up pink. At first it was indistinguishable from the glow of the fires. To the north of us, to the south, to east and to west the horizon was red.

With the coming of daylight even the fires began to look less ominous. In London we had never had a sustained day raid, and we all relegated dangers and horrors to the hours of darkness. Everything would be possible in daylight, the hydrants would miraculously flow with water again, the Rescue men would be able to lift the heavy piles of concrete. The street around us was a sordid mess of piles of bricks and débris, glass, furniture, beams and litter; but as the sun burst over the tops of the ruins, it seemed to wash the dirt away. The cool morning breeze made us feel cleaner ourselves. A nightmare night was over, and a beautiful clear April day was beginning. Fifteen minutes after the sound of the last plane had faded into the distance, the all-clear sounded. Its ugly high-pitched note screamed triumphantly and, for us, seemed to combine the melody of a French horn with the pride and exaltation of twenty thousand roosters.

I thumped George on the back as hard as I could and shouted 'We're still here!' He grinned a little, and said 'Yes; I didn't think we would be, did you?' I had felt so certain that we could not survive till breakfast that I now felt terrifically elated. Despite the misery and the squalor all around, life was wonderful. As soon as the Rescue men who had been working to extricate the old man had signed off, we went back to the Post and had some of Archie's extra strong tea. Izzie told me that my husband had rung through, to ask if I was still about, and had said that the bomb in our square had been on the other side, quite forty yards away. It was nearly 7 a.m. and I forgot that I was tired—I felt fine. As soon as we had cleared up, I should be having breakfast. However, when George suggested that I should clear off then, I did not argue. As I rode off Georgie 2 shouted after me, 'Mind you wash your face before you kiss your old pot and pan, you dirty girl.'

For a great part of the way home I had to carry my bicycle over glass inches deep, and inextricable tangles of hose-pipe; but when I could ride, I rode. The main street was still lined with fires on each side, and smuts and large black flakes were still whirling about; but I shouted good morning to the firemen and they gave a cheer in return. They had had a far more strenuous time than I, but I don't think even they felt tired at that moment. Nearer home the street at the bottom of the hill was flooded; a torrent of water was pouring unchecked into the basements of three small houses, and the tables and chairs were floating and bumping against the ceiling. The street was entirely deserted; but I presumed that someone somewhere must be trying to do something about it, and, too tired to make a detour, waded through.

The damage in our square was not serious. The top floors of two houses had gone and there was a hole in the road exposing a broken sewer. But in the street behind my house there was a dreary sight. Late in the raid three HE's had come down in a cluster, demolished four houses, shattered several others, and blown a huge crater in the middle of the road, bursting a large water main. Eleven people had been crushed and drowned. Reg, the milkman, told me that Wally Marshall and many of the other wardens of Post 2 had done a grand job. They had swum across the crater and into the flooded basements, and had rescued many of the dazed and battered occupants, before the water rose too high. Wally was killed in the next raid, and never knew that he was given the George Medal for his exploits that night. He was a conscientious objector.

When I got home, all the doors and window-frames had gone again. There was no gas, no electricity, worst of all, no water, and I had a tin of beans, cold, with bread and butter, instead of the coffee and sizzling bacon and egg that I had pictured. It is impossible to imagine, in advance, how awkward a total lack of water can be. Candles and lamps can supplant electricity, coal and wood fires can supplant gas, but the lack of water is inordinately inconvenient. I had thought that I did not use much water, but even the worst of housewives has need of it at least thirty times a day.

Later, I went back to the street behind the house to see if I could be of any assistance; but although there were people still buried there, there was no hope at all of their being alive, and there was little one could do. The bodies were not badly mutilated owing to the water and clay. When they reached Mrs. Morland of Number 11 she was lying peacefully on her face, wrapped in a solid pack of wet soft earth. We brought furniture and belongings out of the wrecked houses into the street. One man was having to move for the third time. He had been bombed out by an almost direct hit twice before in different parts of London, and now said he was obviously a Jonah.

A frail and bedraggled old lady came up and begged us to allow her to go back into the tottering remains of her house to fetch Billy. Billy was a tabby, and always refused to leave a cupboard on the top floor during raids. As a rule she stayed with him, terrified though she must have been; but it had been almost morning when the street had been hit, and she had just gone downstairs. The house was extremely unsafe, and it was stupid to take unnecessary risks for a cat, but Mackin, the Post Warden, managed to slip past the Incident Officer unnoticed and fetched it down.

According to the newspapers the Germans were claiming that it had been the greatest raid of all time—so far. Six enemy planes had been shot down, but a thousand men, women and children had been killed, and over two thousand injured. When I reported at my Post that night, all the exultation and pleasure in being alive had gone. As the twilight deepened so did our apprehensiveness. Even Arthur and Stan were 'off their cards' and did not want to play that, or darts. We went along to the pub to get some fortification against another possible nightmare night. We were welcomed, as, at that time, the public sincerely thought that we were 'a good lot.' At 11 p.m. the siren sounded. I caught George's eye, and I don't think that he felt any brighter about the prospect than I did. However, there were only a few planes and nothing happened.

The next night also there was no raid worthy of the name, but on Saturday the planes came again in force. It was a concentrated attack mainly to the east of us, Walthamstow and East Ham way, but we had a handsome share of fires, a few HE's and several UXB's nearby. Our record of the latter was getting somewhat out of hand; when they struck buildings already demolished, or loose piles of débris, they did not leave the neat round hole that they are supposed to make, and it was far from easy to trace them. It was not a pleasant night, but it did not stand comparison with Wednesday's raid.

Sunday was my day 'off,' and I went straight from the Post to the station to see if there were any trains running. The upper floors of the station were still burning, and the platforms were covered with the filthy, slimy oil of several fire bombs, but the 4.30 a.m. was just leaving at 7 a.m., and I slept the whole way to Cambridge. By ill-luck, as I left the train, I met a theatrical company on tour, most of whose members I knew. I was very embarrassed, as I was still in my dusty dungarees and my face was smeared and dirty.

A large friend of mine, in a pale blue spring outfit with grey furs dangling, said 'Good gracious!' when she recognised me. But when I said that we had had a heavy night in London, nobody was interested, and the subject changed to contracts, and how bad poor Peter was in his part. 'But, of course, my dear, as you know, he shouldn't ever have gone on the stage—just hasn't got it in him.' I felt like a foreigner. I had grown so used to old Archie and the Georges that my earlier friends now appeared stranger than Archie had, when I first met him. I could still talk the language, just as I can still recite 'Au clair de la lune . . .' But it did not mean very much.

The provinces certainly suffered from bomb stories, and had a right to be bored with them, as most bomb stories are the same—'I said to Annie, "there's something coming," and we dived under the table.' But there was also a real lack of interest, as well as disbelief. They did not want to be reminded of other people's troubles, the war was going on quite nicely where they were, and that was enough. Later that morning we called in at the George and Dragon. The publican was in his Home Guard uniform, and asked me if we had had a bad night in London. I said, yes, and was going on, when he interrupted and said, 'So have we, and all this morning too. We've been plastered with bombs, plastered with them—mud bombs, of course. But we captured two pubs and drank them dry.' The Home Guard, too, was having a lovely war. However, Londoners did not in their hearts mind the lack of sympathy; we were secretly rather proud of having had a greater tonnage of bombs dropped on us than any city in the world had then had.

We had had the greatest tonnage, and we had had by far the longest endurance tests. But the London warden's chance of survival was much greater than that of his colleagues in Coventry, for instance. London is twenty miles across. When Bristol, Plymouth, Liverpool, and the other big provincial cities were heavily smashed, we in the Civil Defence Services, at least, knew that the nightmare must have been more harrowing than those that we had experienced. In those cities, shelter accommodation was less extensive; the CD Services were less well organised; the defences were not so strong, and the target area could not be compared with our vast space. In London, if one borough was getting more than it could cope with, there was always another fairly close, and fully prepared, to help it out. We felt we were old-timers, and we were genuinely sorry for the new recruits. When, much later, Bath and Norwich 'got it,' several of us wanted to volunteer to help.

For the rest of April we had it fairly quiet. One night, in Bill and Con's, there was a little warden from the next Post, holding forth with the speed and vivacity of Max Miller. I was surprised that I had not met him before, but Georgie was reluctant to introduce me even then. He could not do anything about the dangers of bombs, but he thought he must, at least, protect me from 'doubtful characters.' The man was a first-class showman of the 'Step up—step up and buy my wares' type, with the very fine name of Wellington Everard Dawson, known as Joe, or 'Doc' for short. For years he had been a 'crocus' (the correct and eighteenth-century term for a quack doctor), but he had also been in the circus business, promoted wrestling, and had traded in almost everything. I got to know him well after the raids ceased. The fact that my profession had been in the theatre seemed to cement our acquaintance, even if I had only been concerned with the 'dull' and highbrow side. If any of Joe's friends looked doubtful of talking in front of me, he would glibly say, 'Oh, she's wide all right—show girl.' Alternatively he would introduce me as 'our ginger hell-cat,' and tell a long story about having once found me at the top of a blazing building, trying to drag an unexploded bomb down the fire-escape. I could hardly cap such towering flights of fancy, and would merely smile, modestly. No doubt a number of his other stories had little more resemblance to truth, but they were very exciting.

One evening we met Tiger Bob Newton in the Black Dog, and there followed long reminiscences of Lane's and the wrestling world. Joe told us, and Tiger Bob confirmed it, how he had fought Battling

Bill someone. Like most wrestling, it had all been carefully rehearsed. Joe was to get thrown out of the ring in the first round, to get Bill down in the second, but to get kneed in return. The crowd reacted according to plan, booed Battling Bill, and cheered 'Doc' Joe with gusto, until the glorious climax when Joe's inventive genius brought the curtain down to terrific applause. 'I had two capsules, one in each cheek, my own make, and mine were much harder than anyone else's, I used to bake them in the oven and they'd easily last three rounds, and when I got my teeth into his ear, and all the blood ran down his face—sheep's blood of course—did the boys cheer!'

Once or twice I met him with a fellow 'crocus,' and they would exchange stories of the various lines they had worked. To judge by these, half the world seemed to be peopled by ingenuous fools clamouring to be diddled. However, his 'remedies' often had beneficial results, although this may be difficult to believe. He once charged a farmer an extortionate price for a simple purge and a great deal of alarming sales talk. A month later, when he was doing very well in the market-place of a neighbouring town— 'tosheroons (half-crowns) were rolling in'—this farmer elbowed his way through the crowd. Joe immediately told his mate to start up the car. The farmer shouted that he wanted to take him by the hand, 'but' said Joe, 'I knew that one. They get you by the hand, and the next you know is you're out of the cart on the ground. So I wasn't having any. But you know, that chap, he climbed on the wheel, and shouted, "My friends, my friends, I have been sick and very ill for over ten year now, and this man, he have cured me!" After that, business was better than ever.

He was short, with the india-rubber face of the seasoned music-hall artist, and was crowned with a bush of curly grey hair. He was over fifty and lame in one leg, but it was a great mistake to think that he was easy game in a fight. Sometimes his lameness was due to 'the interests of radiology, my friends,' sometimes, and more probably, to a wound in the last war; but despite it, he was extremely agile. He had an extensive, if inaccurate, vocabulary, and his accounts of crocusing and all its ramifications were fascinating.

It would be out of the question even to imagine Joe non-plussed, or in any way stuck for an answer. Immediately on the issue of gas masks (long before he joined the Wardens' Service) he had had printed a sticky-back, saying 'ARP Anti-Respirator Panic—One in the mouth, and you breathe easily.' It was an ordinary lozenge, but for all that, it sometimes worked, as the act of sucking induced people to stop gasping and breathe normally. If, in a bar, he heard someone say he had an ache, Joe would lean over, tap the man gently on the shoulder, and fixing him with his eye, say, 'Pardon me, sir, did I hear you say you had a pain in your right arm? Rheumatism? Ah, yes, the hospital said neuritis. Ah, yes, neuritis, neuralger, neurasthenica . . . all the same thing. It comes from the Latin, you know—neures, meaning nerves. It's curious now, a friend of mine was suffering with that last week, and he *begged* me to find him something to assuage his agony. Of course, I don't do anything in that line now. And the prices to-day! However . . .'

He was frequently in trouble with the authorities, but invariably sailed through such inconveniences with ease, either by having something on the bloke who had 'mixed' it for him, or by sheer force of personality. He told his story with disarming frankness and great volubility, and few people could muster sufficient wit at the end of his narrative to say they did not believe a word of it.

9

Full Moon Again

As the May moon grew to full we were all expecting trouble. Would it be worse than April had been? By the Thursday of the second week the moon was brilliant. Nothing happened. On Friday it was at its zenith, but again it was quiet. Perhaps, we thought, we might be missed this month. But on Saturday we paid for that faint flicker of optimism.

On the night of the 10th-11th there were 1,436 killed and 1,792 injured, and the attack was distributed over a larger number of districts than previously.

The siren was followed immediately by the drone of many bombers, and there was no doubt in any of our minds that this was going to be a heavy night, at least as heavy as April 16th. To sap one's confidence further, Gloomy Frank was in charge of the Post that night; he was never sure of himself, and naturally, therefore, we had no great faith in him. Harding had the faculty of making up his mind quickly; if he turned out to be wrong, that was unlucky, but it could not be helped and he never havered about. Training may teach one what to do at an incident, but it cannot teach one, when two incidents occur simultaneously, which should receive one's limited attention first. Clearly, residential areas take precedence, but the bomb on the left may have hit a temporarily deserted block of flats, and the one on the right an office or works, where there may be four or five fire-watchers. Harding had always taken the responsibility for such decisions, and we all willingly left it to him, glad to be relieved of the strain of having to think. Poor Frank had none of his assurance and very little of his intelligence, and I knew that before the night was out I should have to make some decisions myself. Into the bargain we were short-staffed. Apart from Harding being away, Izzie and Georgie 2 were having their day off, and though Georgie would certainly turn out as soon as he could, Izzie probably would not. Another was sick, and, to make matters worse, Arthur Purton got hit in the first half-hour. That left us six full-time wardens and two volunteers, one of whom had never been known to put his nose far out of his shelter. It was not a rosy prospect.

At once, the white flickering of hundreds of incendiaries started in Cannon Street direction, accompanied by the red flaring of several oil bombs. That was going to be a Number 1 Fire, and although it was some distance from us, it was near enough for us to get the 'misses' if the Ack-Ack was going to be heavy protecting the firemen working on it. Two HEs arrived, one on the station, five minutes' walk away, and one close, close enough for the dust to reach us. Frank called me to go with him to see where it was. I was surprised, as he had always made it abundantly clear that he had no use for females.

Each person develops his own technique in raids. Both Frank and Tiny dodged into doorways, or lay flat, too often for my taste. In reality I had less 'courage' than either of them but although it was a fairly sensible precaution I found that, for me, it increased my general nervousness, and after the first three weeks I never lay down as long as I could hear a bomb whistle. In all, I only went flat intentionally three times. As we walked the air grew thicker with dust, till we could hardly see. It was as thick as a bad London fog, but the damage was across the border, and even if the other wardens had needed it we dared not offer assistance off our own ground so early in the night.

On the way back there was a fierce burst of gunfire nearby, directed at one of the planes heading our way, followed a few seconds later by a furiously urgent sound like an express train entering a tunnel. Without a word we both went flat on our faces in the gutter. Instinctively I got a good hold of a lamp-post base, and noted with satisfaction that we were alongside an old crater—there would be no seven storeys to fall on us. The bombs came down in a cluster, close together, on the drill hall the other side of the road. Bomb explosions have a mesmeric attraction dating possibly from firework displays of one's childhood, and I watched the first two explode. Unless it lifts an entire building in the air, the burst of an ordinary high explosive bomb is not in itself a grand spectacle, as a major fire can be; its upward streaks of yellow or red look as crude and banal as a small boy's painting of them.

After the second burst, my discretion returned and I buried my face in my arms; it is ridiculous to risk facial injury unnecessarily. I could not count the explosions, but there were three or four more. 'Control,' for excellent statistical reasons, always wants to know exactly how many bombs there have been, but unless they fell fifty yards apart my ears could never distinguish the number at close quarters. Then, there are only two things that matter: the fact that you have not yourself been hit yet, and possible other casualties. The blast came along with a rush and a bang, but the lamp-post and the kerb were a protection and the gap in the buildings on our left let it rush by. A brick hit me on the thigh with some force, and the glass fell out of the windows, but there was very little glass left.

When I stood up Frank had disappeared; he had been almost touching my feet, and as he must be, surely, a little heavier than myself, I could hardly believe that he had been blown away. However, I found him round the corner. Almost without his own knowledge he had got up and moved. 'I dunno how I got there,' he said. We congratulated each other on our luck, and our mutual respect increased considerably. We were not allowed long, however,

for in less than a minute an extensive shower of incendiaries rained down ahead of us along the street, as far as we could see. Some struck buildings, many fell around our wooden Post. Here came the first awkward decision: should we deal with the fire bombs, several of which were in dangerous positions, or should we go to the drill hall? If there were only minor injuries the soldiers could surely deal with those themselves, and one had the illogical feeling also that the military could not ever need mere civilian assistance.

Frank ran off after the incendiaries. I, as usual, hesitated. I found two sand-bags at the foot of a lamp-post, solid with the attentions of countless dogs, and dumped them on the nearest bombs while I made up my mind. At that second an entire shop window was suddenly lit up. The owner leant through where the glass had been and inanely enquired where the bombs had fallen. He refused to put out the light and we had a furious altercation, before I walked off angrily to the drill hall. Fire had broken out there and it was impossible to see which part of the place had been hit.

I found that there was no sentry at the gate, and that decided me: there must be fairly serious trouble. As I got near to the fire there was a lot of shouting and running about, and a soldier called to me, 'Hi! mate, get us an ambulance, there's a lot underneath.' I asked if there were more than six, and ran off while he was still apologising for having misjudged my sex.

It is a great mistake for anyone without exceptionally good wind to run: far better to be strong-minded, as Harding had been, and walk; at moments of urgency he would rise to a lolloping, though dignified trot, but no more. Once one starts to run one must keep it up. My heavy leather coat seemed to weigh a hundredweight. It clung round my knees and prevented them moving, my haversack, with respirator and first-aid essentials, bumped up and down in a contrary rhythm, I felt as if my chest was being crushed in, and there was not enough room in my mouth for my enormous tongue.

As I reached the Post I was greeted with another hailstorm of incendiaries. Frank was busy with a stirrup pump on a fire on the first floor of a house, and shouted something through a gap in the wall, but I hadn't the breath even to say 'What?' and thought that in any case the report came first. There was an incendiary on the steps of the pill-box, I put a sand-bag on it and stepped over, hoping that one of the others would not trip over it and break his neck, and went to phone. At first I could not get the dialling tone, then I tried three of the Control numbers and could not get a sound; at the fourth I got the right ringing noise and it went on and on and no reply came. It was a wrong number, a private house, and the owner was unjustifiably annoyed.

It took minutes to disconnect and I began to think it would be better to be coping with fire-bombs than playing about with a recalcitrant telephone. An incoming call held me up further. This was the proprietor of the Dog and Duck telling me that Warden Purton had been hit in the neck and was bleeding profusely. At last I got through, told the girl that I had two express and one MI report. But here was more ill-luck: she was evidently new at the work, and as I started '13D reporting . . .' I heard her say, 'Wait a minute, while I get my pad.' I waited and began again. 'Wait a minute, I haven't got the carbons in.' I told her to hold on at all costs and dashed upstairs to see how the fires were getting on. Two were getting on rather too well, and someone shouted that we should need the Fire Brigade. I got back to the phone and asked the girl if she was ready by now, only to be greeted with 'Wait a minute,'I can't find my pencil.' Exasperated is too mild a word, I felt frantic and powerless, and wanted to yell, but just managed to give the reports very slowly, one word at a time; she did not know the district and the names of the streets had each to be spelt. While she passed on the two expresses I had another look at the fires, and changed the third report to a supplementary, saying that a shower of incendiaries had fallen but was now under control.

Stan arrived and reported the drill hall incident and Purton's injury. He had approached from the other side and had more details; there were ten buried. Frank and Georgie 2 went off with the incident lamps to the barracks, and old Archie and Tiny to see if the people in their shelters were safe. We none of us saw these two again until 3 a.m., which reduced our mobile strength to five.

My chief impression of the whole of that night is one of chaos; throughout the five or six hours when it was at its height, there was repeatedly the need to be in two places at once. Twice in the next hour, while I was the only warden in the eastern half of our area (and this was quite a quarter of a mile square), I had to go and investigate HE's, and leave no one at the Post. The rules say that the Post telephone must always be manned, but this was out of the question. The telephone itself continued to be exasperating, until at 1.30 a.m., after a heavy crash not far away, it went completely dead. In one way it was a relief; it certainly saved my temper, but it meant that now we should have to go all the way to Post 12 with reports.

Billy Barker came up breathlessly and said that Tasker Street block of flats had been hit for a second time, but without casualties, and that as he was coming to the Post the block in Durlin Street had been hit, and there were two killed and some hurt. I asked Billy to go to the barracks, find Frank or Georgie, and get one of them to take charge of Durlin Street. For the first and last time while I was at Post 13 an Incident Officer from the Town Hall had shown up at the drill hall incident. But he seemed to want to get back to the Town Hall as quickly as possible, and declined to take over a second incident without official instructions. I went off to '12.'

Fires were everywhere; the one in Cannon Street now looked nearly a mile long; to the south of that there was a vast conflagration at the Elephant. As I went along the main road, lifting my bicycle over tangles of hose-pipe, piles of débris and glass, about every third turning was blazing. We had sweated and struggled with repeated loads of incendiaries, and got them under control, all to no purpose: down came an oil bomb and the whole building would go up in flames.

I passed Condon Street and Feather Street; on both sides flames were pouring out of the empty windows like Atlantic breakers on the Cornish coast. One building was producing vivid green and blue flames, another, a paper manufacturing firm, was sending off long sheets of flaming paper; they hovered over the street, buoyed up by the hot air, suddenly died out and dissolved into black flakes tossed in all directions by the tornado below. To face this holocaust there were seven or eight appliances and many dozen firemen—but no water. Firemen were standing with the branches under their arms, and only a trickle of water was dripping on to their boots. They looked hopeless and beaten; they were well trained, efficient and courageous, but without water they might just as well have stayed in their stations as stand, unwillingly idle, round fires that always attracted high explosives.

In our area we had always suffered from a shortage of water from the City fire onwards, but to-night it was worse than ever. All over

133

London, because there was no water, fires which could easily have been controlled by one or two pumps, had to be allowed to engulf the whole street. Fires and huge HE's were the distinguishing marks of the night. The throb of planes never stopped, every few minutes bombs whistled down all around us, and exploded with a shattering roar.

When I got back to our Post an oil bomb had fallen on a building thirty yards away, and four floors were blazing. Fire-watchers had already informed the Fire Brigade. I decided that I could not keep going to '12,' and that I would wait and take three reports together unless there were living casualties. This new fire was uncomfortably close to the Post, and was spreading rapidly, although, in this case, there was, intermittently, a small supply of water. A firework display of shrapnel twinkled overhead. But shrapnel was one of the things about which we had all very quickly developed the old soldier's knowledgeableness, and I duly crossed the road and stood in a doorway, till the bits came down with their sighing whistle, and tinkled on the pavements. Still, I thought, it meant that our fire was looking quite attractive from up above—attractive enough to merit some high explosive.

To divert my uneasy attention from it I watched the Cannon Street blaze. As I watched, a plane dropped six whistling HE's into the middle of it, and a burst of flame shot up to a huge height. I was wondering how many firemen had gone under with that 'packet,' and whether our fire would be the next, when Stan arrived and said that two HE's had fallen in Market Street, wrecked four or five of the little shops, and Sammy Western and all his family of ten were buried.

Suddenly I remembered the telephone in the shelter under the insurance building, which Harding and I had used before. It would be much quicker than going to '12,' and I hurried there. They had a good fire of their own burning on the top floor, but they had an efficient fire party, hydrants and full-sized hose, and had not notified us. Water was cascading down the marble stairs. The fire-party captain told me that he thought the phone was still working, but when I got downstairs I found that it also had failed. The shelterers asked me how it was going up above. It was an excellent shelter, air-conditioned and with steel doors which made it sound-proof, and all the children were sleeping peacefully as though nothing at all was happening overhead. They offered me a cup of tea, but although it was a great temptation, I had already wasted time, and I set off for '12.' I decided to make a small detour through Market Street and when I got there I found that Frank and Georgie had already sent a report from '12.'

These two had had a frenzied time on their side: countless incendiaries, many oil bombs, several HE's, a shelter flooded with water from the hoses, while there still had been some water—and an altercation. The altercation had been unpleasant and stormy. When Frank had reached the incident, a man's body had been lying in the road for ten minutes, so he moved it under cover. Shortly after, the corpse's brother-in-law came straight up to Frank and accused him of taking £5 from the deceased's pocket. Frank rightly retorted, how the hell did he know there was any b——£5 in the deceased's pocket? It was unthinkable that Frank would rob a corpse, particularly that of a man whom he knew, and he was probably right in thinking that the brother-in-law had done it himself, and needed to find a scapegoat before he faced his sister. But it was unpleasant; there was trouble enough with the Germans without having a local war as well.

Sammy Western's incident was tragic. He was a popular little man, and a small crowd of relatives and friends had come out of the shelters to stand anxiously by while the Heavy Rescue got to work. Women were crying quietly, and everyone seemed to have told Sammy only that evening that 'he never ought to stay in that house of his': it was old and flimsy, and there was also danger of flooding in the basement. A danger that had materialised.

I went back to the Post but I was growing very tired of my own company. I had been alone, either near the Post or on my bicycle, for two hours, except for short visits from Billy and Stan, and I had diminishing confidence in my ability. Some voluntary wardens from the next borough turned up and told me that there was an unexploded oil bomb on our side of the dividing road. I felt that even if they must keep up the 'border war' they could at least have left us in ignorance until the morning, but I thanked them as politely as I could. It was on Archie's sector, and for nearly four hours he had been down one of his shelters. No doubt he would turn up with a story of how panicky all the shelterers had been, but I was tired; we had had far too many bombs that night, and I could not get up any interest in one that had not ignited, and even if it did—what would one more fire matter when we already had so many? So I found Archie and asked him to go and cover it with wet sand in case other incendiaries came down near it. It was not, in fact, my business to tell anybody to do anything, but on a night as chaotic as this, points of etiquette had to go by the board, and, grumbling, old Archie went. Archie's defection was not as inexcusable as it may sound: none of the bombs till now had been actually on his sector; he was over fifty and lame and, more important, he had always 'worked' on his own and was not imbued with any notions about public spirit or communal welfare.

By 4 a.m. the raid was getting less intense. There were gaps between the planes now, and one began to hope that in an hour, with luck, it might be over. Frank and Georgie came back, and when Archie returned from his oil bomb he made some badly needed tea for us all. We had a welcome half-hour's relaxation, during which everyone began to relate his particular bomb stories, hot from the press. Even when they had been at the same incident the stories were entirely different. Events on one side of a crater are not at all the same as those on the other. Our interval was terminated abruptly by yet another oil bomb on a firm two hundred yards away, and close to an existing fire; it was the only part of that street that was as yet unburnt, and now it was blazing fiercely. The firemen did their best with a miserably low pressure of water, but a little later with a resounding crash the building fell in, burying two of the crew. Their bones were not found till three months later.

At 5 a.m. a warden from '12' rode up with a message from Control that we were 'to immediately send a complete report of all damage, particularly to business premises.' We were indignant. For one thing, the raid was not over yet; in fact, we were still to get one more HE; and though we were all willing to take chances when lives were concerned, we were not prepared to take these chances for the sake of a red-tape survey. For another thing, we resented the emphasis on *business* premises. Herbert Morrison had only recently reasserted the prime importance of preventing fires in business premises, but it had cut little ice with us, as we felt that the Salvage Officers and the owners and the insurance companies would settle that side of the matter for themselves. Lastly, we felt that it could at least wait until the day shift came on. They would be comparatively

House facades sliced away by bombs in the night

fresh, while we were jaded. So for three good reasons we agreed unanimously to refrain from any immediate or hasty action.

For the next hour I was too tired to be fully conscious of anything that might be going on. But at 6 a.m., when the all-clear went, I started off on the tour of inspection of damage. Many of the fires were now only smouldering and smelt evilly, but a large number were still blazing and roaring. The streets looked dreary and desolate. The centre of one block had been sliced out and most of the rubble lay in the road where two surface shelters had been. The mortuary van had not yet come to remove Frank's contentious corpse. A few women were standing wearily in the street, listlessly watching their husbands poking about in the débris, unearthing bits of iron bedsteads, small personal treasures, or unrecognisable furnishings. They were pale and unkempt, and their bodies had a dejected helpless droop—they looked so tired that never again would they be able to summon any energy. I gave them all the information I could about the Rest Centres, and the Mayor's fund, etc., but with a listless 'Thanks' they went on staring at the ruins of what had been their homes.

For the well-to-do, the ruin of a home may be a serious financial loss, and a loss of many personal treasures, but there is always a bank balance, and usually insurance; but for many of the poor it is a disaster only comparable with the loss of life. For many wives, their home had been their life's work. All their energy, all their attention, for thirty years had gone into polishing, patching and scrubbing; they went without luxuries to get the furniture, they spent years paying for it, and now that furniture which was almost a part of them is a pile of splinters. The face of one woman was purple with crying, and the tears streamed down her cheeks, but she made no noise.

At Sammy Western's they were still digging. I asked a man whom I only knew as Bert, and who was watching operations in a detached and idle manner, how many were still underneath. He replied, 'My sister's still there, and her baby, George and Elsie, and Sammy; my other brother was got out, but he was dead, his wife's all right.' I could think of no condolences to fit such a catalogue of disaster.

Our inventory of damage took a long time. Control wanted the names of all firms affected: it was no use to say, 'The whole of Feather Street gone.' Georgie was far better at it than I was, but even he found it difficult to remember all the names, when a long stretch of street had been demolished. When it was finished, I went off to see if the local baths were giving any service and whether there was any food to be had. The day shift had taken over some time before.

Considerably later I re-visited the Post and was greeted by Charlie with a message that Warden Nixon was to be transferred back to Post 2. I was furious. I might not have wanted to go to '13' in the first place, but in the five months that I had been there I had grown very attached to them, dirty old Archie and gloomy Frank included. Frank said he was going to protest, but Charlie interrupted, 'You know they've been hit—the Post I mean; half of them have been killed.' I knew that there had been a bomb in the square where the Post was; '12' had told me that on one of my reporting visits, but they had already had two oil bombs there which had given no serious trouble, and, altogether illogically, I had assumed that it was only another. My stomach turned horribly cold and heavy and I kicked myself for having wasted so much time.

I set off on my bike, pedalling hard, and speculating futilely as to which members of the Post had been unlucky. As I reached my 'local' I saw that it was open, and went in to ask Tom and Milly if they knew which of the wardens had been killed; I did not want to make the same blunder that I had made at Sammy Western's. Tom gave me nine or ten names. 'It's a shame,' said Milly. 'We've lost some lovely people.' I met the occupants of the flat above mine and they told me that our house was done for. This, I found later, was an exaggeration.

Survivors were standing around in clusters, all of them were an ochre colour from head to foot, from the yellowish brick dust; it matted their hair, penetrated their skins, and their clothes; washing would not remove the colour, and in any case there was no water except from an emergency stand-pipe. Tom and Milly had opened their doors 'out of hours,' and stood nearly half their stock. People were making arrangements to go to the mortuary to identify bodies, and so save the most direct relatives from further shock. The mortuary always did its best to make corpses presentable, but it was no easy task; in many cases there was not sufficient left to make it possible, and sometimes they fitted the wrong pieces together. But for the widows and parents, it was the greatest service one could render.

Overleaf: The rescue squads at work amidst a mass of debris and at close quarters, freeing a woman who was buried up to her neck in rubble

10

Aftermath

ALL through the blitzes we had regarded 2 as a 'lucky' and relatively safe area, but now that myth had been exploded in one gross catastrophe. Even on this night there had been no incidents until ten minutes to two. The only entry in the log-book was a message sent by the Post Warden—his last message—asking for a doctor to be sent to a sick baby in a shelter. But at 1.50 two enemy objects dropped close together, exploded on the surface, and blasted two squares and the streets leading out of them. They had been pleasant squares, built about 1840, a little shabby now, but with large rooms and windows and each with its own garden. If the inhabitants of Bloomsbury had known of their existence they might have invaded them, but as it was, the original inhabitants continued in residence; for the most part, these held steady comfortable jobs in the post office, the police, the railways, etc.

Now, many of the houses had disappeared entirely: the remainder were only battered skeletons. Trees were lying uprooted, scorched, blackened and half-buried by piles of bricks and chimneys, baths and doors, and here and there a battered tin hat. Post 13 had been far more widely devastated, but the devastation was chiefly of business premises. The ruins of Holford Street had a more intimate desolation. A child's toy caught on the twisted railings, a perambulator hurled into a fantastic position, a cooking-stove hanging in mid-air, supported apparently only by the gas-pipe, a chair with a man's Sunday suit neatly folded over the back, balancing on the edge of a severed upper floor, the patchwork of different coloured wall-papers on the exposed walls; it all showed the ruin of so many personal lives.

Of the wardens, Mackin the Post Warden, Marshall, who had behaved so gallantly in the last blitz, and George Palser, had been killed outright. Johnny Trew died next day, a piece of railing had

'. . . the ruin of so many personal lives . . .'

blown into his stomach. His brother was in hospital seriously burnt; most of the others were suffering from acute blast effects, and were deaf from pierced ear-drums. Mackin, Wally Marshall and George had been standing outside the pill-box, and why they did not hear or see the thing coming, remains a mystery. Mrs. Hughes, standing in a doorway thirty yards away, had heard the first one, and had yelled. Others had had time at least to lie flat. Perhaps they saw it at the last moment coming straight at them and were too paralysed to move—the steps down to the pill-box were too narrow to take all three of them, and there was no other cover. In any case, it can only have been a second or so of despair. Their friends told us that the two RAF men killed had gone to the door to find out what the curious noise was—and just as they reached the entrance the first went off. The final figure of killed was fifty-two, including the four wardens, two policemen, and two airmen; the injured were well over a hundred, though only forty-six were detained in hospital more than one night.

At first there was chaos. Our records of the residents had gone with the Wardens' Post, the Post Warden was dead, his deputy happened to be on six days' leave; most of the other wardens had been blown varying distances, and were stupefied and literally deafened by the noise; many of their homes had been destroyed. Inevitably there had been confusion. One of the Incident Officers had tried to get a message to me three times during the early morning, as I knew the people and the district, but our telephone at '13' was out of action and no messenger came. By the time that I arrived, most of those who could be hoped to be alive had been rescued. A little girl of six or seven, blinded and shockingly cut by glass, was got out, but her parents were both dead. At '13' the reverse had happened, a man and his wife had escaped but their baby had been killed, and the woman had run screaming desperately up and down the street. But there is no logic or equity in bombing. All that week the Rescue Party went on digging, patiently and carefully. Often the only clue that we had that someone was still buried was the smell that seeped up from the blocked basements.

All that was left of the Post was the sunk concrete pill-box. The house in which the Post proper had been was cut in half, but the pill-box had stood the blast amazingly well. There was a crater ten feet deep directly beside it, but even the telephone survived in working

The gentle rescue of an elderly man

order. Some of the younger voluntary messengers hung up a faded Union Jack, and the respirators and tin hats of the dead wardens. These scorched and eyeless respirators under their twisted helmets looked like mutilated faces, and gave a horribly macabre effect.

Nearby was a steel-boned corset which we had salvaged: it belonged to an elderly humpty-backed man, and though we did not know whether he was alive or dead, such things are expensive, and he was far from rich. It, too, looked very pathetic. He was a quiet retiring man, who walked bent double over two sticks, but was still working as a draughtsman, and could throw a dart underhand with surprising accuracy. Ever since he had come to our district I had had a mild and bitter with him on Friday evenings at Tom and Milly's. He told me that his house in Westminster had been hit, and he had been buried for twelve hours. Now his home had been hit again. We tried to trace him from hospital to hospital, but unless one is a near relative it is not a simple proceeding, and we had no success. In any case it did not seem possible that so frail and bent a body could survive such a furious tornado of blast.

Eighteen months later I suddenly saw him, hobbling along a street. He had just come out of hospital, where he had lain all those months with both arms suspended on pulleys to the ceiling. He looked older and the creases in his thin face were deeper, but he was the most uncomplaining bomb victim that I have met.

We had no Post. In the pill-box there was only room for three sitting and two standing. The Town Hall said we could use public shelters at night, but we did not greatly appreciate the suggestion. It was not possible to smoke, and in any case visiting a shelter and having a chat for ten minutes is quite a different matter from staying there for two hours. After two weeks they allocated to us a shelter whose entrance had been blown in, but which was safe enough; but even then there was no heating in it. So, in the meanwhile, we rigged up a tarpaulin cover outside the pill-box, and as, luckily, the weather was getting warmer, it was soon possible to sleep out of doors under it. It had not ever occurred to me that one would ever sleep out in a London street, but the blitzes caused more surprising changes in one's habits than that.

By day we maintained a roaring wood fire of roof timbers, stair-cases, broken doors, and old tarry road blocks. Eventually we built ourselves a hut out of débris wood. As we were not too certain of our material, or of the principles of strutting and strains, we built it round the trunk of a tree. When finished it looked rather like an alpine goatherd's chalet, with foliage sticking out of the roof, hiding a chimney made out of a loose piece of drain-pipe. But that was not until the autumn.

In the meantime we led a curious life for twentieth-century Londoners. We were never clean. When the Rescue workers finished, the demolition workers came. We sat outside the pill-box in a permanent fog of gritty dust. Every so often there would be a crash and another wall would come down and add further clouds to the existing fog. We drank endless cups of black tea to quench the dust in our throats. At almost any time of the day or night you would usually find at least two or three of us standing about with a mug in our hands. When finished you tipped the dregs into the roadway, dipped the mug into the dirtier of the two buckets, and waited until the next spoonful was added to the sodden mass of tea-leaves already half-filling the pot. The habit became so strong that on one of my Sundays off, in Cambridge, standing in front of the fireplace, cup and saucer in hand, I jerked the tea leaves on to the carpet, in a sudden and astonished silence.

When the sun shone we sweated, and clean trickles meandered down our faces; when it rained, one's complexion looked more like a mud-pack. We abandoned any pretence at washing: in two minutes we were as filthy as before. The nearest water was a stand-pipe a hundred yards away, and we fetched it in two bucketfuls at a time— one for what was called washing up, the other to go in the kettle for tea.

My own house though still 'habitable' was well messed up. Five ceilings had come down, either in part or entirely, all window-frames and doors were out, and two interior walls had gone; it was no longer necessary to open the door leading into the main room; even if it had been there, it was just as easy to walk through the wall. The bath was full of bricks, the beds and floors were covered with plaster, laths and glass. The other occupants had moved out, and it was not worth while tackling the job of clearing up, as the emergency repair workers would have to come in, and they always made nearly as much mess as another bomb. Clothes, carpets, curtains, blankets, everything was thick with brick and plaster dust.

I applied to the Mayor's Fund. (A female warden's wage was

then £2 7s. 6d. a week.) I postponed going for three or four days as there were hundreds of others who were in far worse case than I was, but when I got there I was sent on to the Public Assistance Committee. I reached the PAC at ten minutes to four; a notice stated that it was open till five, but the officials said they were not taking any more cases and I was to go again next day. I went during the midday break, and after waiting fifty minutes was told that I was in the wrong queue. On my third visit I was told that I must produce the cleaners' bills *before* I could make a claim. But in that case, if I spent £10, I might only get a grant of £5, and the cleaners would not be satisfied with that. In my somewhat jaded and post-blitz state I decided that I preferred dirt to red tape, and weakly abandoned the attempt. I had made the mistake of going in my dirty, warden's dungarees.

Working men and women had to lose a day's pay to get to the PAC while it was open, but that was not the worst fault. The Public Assistance officials could not rid themselves of the idea that they were dispensing charity, and it was this attitude that caused even more resentment and anger than the delays. Even in peace-time it was inexcusable. Since industry seemed to need a reserve of unemployed from which to draw, the unlucky ones who had to form that reserve had a right to some livelihood; it was seldom a man's own fault that he was out of work, still less was it his fault that a Nazi bomb had demolished his home and destroyed all his possessions and means of living. To have his pride trampled on as well, by being treated as a beggar lucky to receive alms, was unforgivable.

The funerals of our fellow-wardens were a greater strain than the blitz itself. At first, the Town Hall made no official preparations for the burial of five of their service members—four wardens and one stretcher-party man—killed on duty. We made eight visits to various officials before they agreed to give municipal support to the arrangements the different families had already made. It was not that we ourselves wanted a 'fuss,' but for most relatives anything that can even make a pretence that their irreparable loss was worthwhile, or that it meant something to others as well as themselves, was at least a slight softening of their bitterness. And there was bitterness. There was still no real war; it seemed we would never be fighting back, and no war could ever be won by sitting down and 'taking it' as the press still encouragingly called it.

Moreover, there had been more in the air than mere high explosive on the last Saturday raid. The same night Hess had landed in Scotland, and was being fed on chicken and grapes, the papers said, because he had broken his ankle. A legion of theories and rumours spread about: some people were optimistic and thought it meant that Germany was cracking up, most were distrustful of the 'high-ups' in this country, a very few hazarded the opinion that the Germans were going to turn against Russia and wanted us out of it. But the upshot was always the same—a gloomy shrug, and 'If we're going to be sold out by Quislings in the end, why put up with all the bombing now?'

At the last moment the Town Hall authorised an official Civil Defence parade for the funerals, and lent us clean overalls for the two days. Members of all our services turned out and lined the streets, and did a slow march to the different churches five times in two days. I am sentimental, bordering on maudlin, by nature, and despite terrific efforts to think of something else, sniffed abominably. I was well jeered at for it by my old tough friends of '13,' who were evidently surprised.

But even the funerals would not go 'according to plan.' With poor Mackin's nothing would go right. He was a Communist, and at first there was delay because official stomachs could not digest the red cotton hearse cloth which his family provided, and justifiably insisted on. At the very last second, as we all about-faced, three young friends of his, who had obviously taken half an hour from work and run most of the way, arrived with a pathetic little bunch of red tulips. Despite the coachman's disapproval, they were fixed in position, and nodded and flopped proudly and jauntily in front of the grand official wreath.

When we halted at Mrs. Trew's house to pick up Johnny (the one who had had the railings blown into him) the hearse became blocked in a cul-de-sac caused by débris, and took over an hour to be extricated. Then, to make up time, Mackin's hearse dashed off through North London to the crematorium at sixty miles an hour, and six of us in a stretcher-car, who were to be bearers, lost it and arrived too late. His requiem—the Internationale—as played by the organist, was unrecognisable, since the latter had never heard the tune before and had a limited mastery of his instrument. It was all dreadful. The only alleviation of one's misery was the thought that

Mackin himself would have had a first-class laugh, saying that he had been a thorn in the flesh of the authorities all his life, and could still make them uncomfortable, even with his feet gone and a hole in his head.

He was a great loss to the Warden's Service; he had been slap-dash in his organisational work at times, but when he was convinced that a grievance was justifiable he was extremely pertinacious in getting it righted, and no authorities could cow him. He was often dogmatic in his arguments, but no one doubted his sincerity, and even those who disagreed violently with his political views had, nevertheless, a great respect for him.

To and from the crematorium North London traffic seemed to almost consist entirely of hearses—grand ones with four horses and nodding plumes, poorer ones with only two horses and no plumes, motorised ones that speeded along. Despite the solemnity of the black mourning, there was an atmosphere of haste. The undertakers were overworked.

At the end of the week the exodus from our district began. Light vans, borrowed from the local tradesmen, hand-barrows, coal carts, assembled in front of the shattered houses. Each day three or four families moved off; they had found a flat or rooms in another part of London, and they dragged or drove their broken furniture away, unwilling to go, hating to leave the house they had lived in for twenty or thirty years, and their local friends and acquaintances.

The community was breaking up. Even Tom and Milly left us. The birds too—the pigeons and the sparrows—seemed to disappear for a time. Curiously enough there had been an owl in the vicinity during the preceding three or four weeks which had hooted and swooped among the trees in Lloyd Square. Perhaps it had been an omen; it was certainly as out of place in London as the one in *Julius Caesar* which sat 'even at noon-day in the market-place, hooting and shrieking.' In any case it must either have been blown to bits or flown silently away. We never heard it again. At the Post we began to think that we should soon be the sole survivors in this desolate land; and as the people went, the rats and the mice moved in. Large sewer rats whose homes had been burst open just as ours had, and hungry mice deserted by their former patrons, swarmed about the ruins and into any house where there was still a tenant to provide for them.

For some, furniture, effects – some connection with former lives – could be saved; for others, the past had disappeared and the future was blank

Not for four weeks did a CD officer from the Town Hall visit us. It was two months before the Chief Warden called. Our only company was occasional police and the demolition workers. The police patrol was doubled in an attempt to stop looting, without much noticeable success. It was an eerie and a dismal patrol for them, and they welcomed our cups of tea, and in return would often, unofficially, light the fire for us as soon as the dawn came up. It improved our relations with the police considerably. Before, anyone who took a policeman into a Post was usually told to choose some other friends, but a year later we were playing them amicably at darts or cricket, despite occasional asides as a batsman came in, that 'that was the guy who ran in Bertie Simmons.'

We did not have a great respect for the demolition workers. The 'top-men' were skilled, and risked their necks on the perilously insecure roof tops to collect the lead in the interests of national economy. But even their efforts were nullified. One evening just after 'knocking-off' time a five-ton lorry drove up, loaded the six-foot high pile of lead from the road, and drove off. Some of this lead, and some of the furniture from our square, was found by the police five months later at an auction sale in Norfolk, along with a great deal of other stolen property.

The majority of the workers were unskilled; they had been directed to the job by the Labour Exchange, with no regard for their fitness for it. There was a little Italian jeweller who had lost his wife, his daughter and his house in a raid, and whose son had been killed with the Eighth Army: he was a pathetic figure, old, broken and frail, and utterly unfit for the work.

Most demolition work was contracted out to house-breaking firms, and in this case everyone knew that the boss had made over the business to his twenty-six-year old son, to save the latter from the army. The longer the job lasted, the more profits there would be, and there was only a poor pretence at checking idling, long lunch breaks and absenteeism. From Friday to Tuesday, fifty per cent would be consistently drunk. They slept it off, and gambled, in the ruined basements: once, the tea-boy, aged about fourteen, received his wages with the rest at midday, and by 8 p.m. had been fleeced of the entire sum at cards. There was no traffic through the square, as it was well concealed from main roads; and several houses which, if barricaded off, could easily have been left standing till after the war, were demolished in order to spin out the job. The demolition men kept cutting their hands; we bandaged them up till our supplies ran out. We applied for replacements of first-aid equipment, but none came and we had to buy stuff ourselves.

The piles of furniture in the square grew in size—piles of bedsteads, battered pianos, sofas, children's stamp albums, dozens of clocks all with their hands standing at ten minutes to two. There were insufficient tarpaulins, and as the weeks dragged by, the rain soaked into the dust-covered upholstery, and the sun, when it deigned to appear, warped the woodwork and faded the colours.

Often in the early morning soldiers and sailors would arrive back on leave. The soldiers had sometimes been notified of their disaster, and came 'just to see if there were any bits left worth having'; but for most of the sailors it was a terrible shock. They had travelled all night to be with their families for breakfast, and found no family and no home. They would wait, silent and gloomy, while we checked the mortuary and hospital lists; if the names were not there, we could give them no other help: only three, out of all the families that had moved, had left any address. We watched them walking miserably away, to fill in the hours before the offices opened which might be able to trace their relatives.

During the first week or so we enjoyed a macabre publicity value; sightseers would ask the police at the nearest railway station the way to the worst bomb damage. Most of us resented it horribly. We preferred our isolation.

Our dreariness was lightened a little by the appointment of one new warden, to make up our losses. He had had no training at all, not even the sketchy amount that we had received. He had never been out in a blitz, had religious mania, and was a refugee of some years standing. On a wet day he would turn up with his beret, which he always wore right down over his eyebrows and ears, covered by his tin hat, and the whole surmounted by an umbrella. He would never take his boots off for his rest at night, but brought two shoe-bags, such as children use to take their slippers to a party, and tied them round his legs. He was a very kindly man, and absurdly generous to various charities, but he knew nothing at all about civil defence. When we asked him what he would do about a fire, he thought hard and then said, 'Oh yez, yez, I would run into ze burning houses, and take all ze names and addresses of ze burning peoples before zay vent; zen oh yez, yez, I would run back into ze burning houses, and turn off all ze dirty water taps.'

One morning he went rather too far, and informed us that he would be quite safe from bombs because bombs only fell on the wicked, not on the good. I was about to retort angrily about the baby in No. 11, but old Heinz, our Czech, lost his usually benign temper and flew at the other, shouting with his equally execrable English, 'You insult my friend Mackin . . . you insult my friend Mr. Marshall!. . . it iz ze fascismus.' And the two old men milled round the Post, grabbing each other by the collar, their foreign accents becoming more and more unintelligible. Nobody intervened. We were too miserable to be more than aware of the funny side of it. He used to read the Bible or religious pamphlets most of the day, and young Joe, the tea-boy, took a wicked delight in asking him to explain the infallibility of passages, such as 'an eye for an eye' and 'turn the other cheek.' He was, however, or became, an expert cleaner of lamps: never had our lamps gleamed so brightly.

Occasionally there were sirens. You could feel the atmosphere of nervousness; few of the wardens said anything about it openly, but there was none of the old excitement and expectation of action. We all dreaded that the night might turn into another May 10th, and that we would not be able to stand up to it. The shelterers were frankly frightened, their hands shook, and a few would stand there crying, even when there was no gunfire or aircraft to be heard.

Depression settled over London, all the more serious in that it was not particularly vocal. Active grumbling or railing was not much heard; small crowds would listen to street speakers and agree with the abuses being pilloried, but what could they do about it? What difference did it make, anyway? What was it all for? For a defeat in Greece—heroic, but a second Dunkirk? Or for an equally heroic débâcle in Crete? In the shelters, the raucous gramophones were silent; there were few attempts to sing or talk; the people sat silently and miserably. A mood of depression can be more dangerous than anger, and had Goering known how strong that mood was, he might well have strained every nerve to continue the aerial bombardment.

The people of London were not cowards. Had there been an invasion there would have been no talk of giving in. Had there been a more active and a more hopeful battle-front, there would have been no depression. But to be forced to sit down under prolonged bombardment with no hope of retaliation, is the hardest sort of war to fight, unless there is a constant and a burning conviction evident. But, even the respite from raids might only be due to Hess and quisling machinations. Mr. Churchill's assurance of complete, absolute, and final victory was not disbelieved, but it seemed as remote and unobtainable as the traditional pie in the sky—there was no road that led there.

At last, on June 16th, my six days' leave was due. I stole two hours of my night duty, did not stop to change my clothes, and caught the 6.30 a.m. train to the Cotswolds. It was a grey morning; the weather had been wet and cold for weeks. At Swindon I noticed two rifts in the overcast sky that might almost be called blue. At Kemble, it was bright blue with snow-white piles of clouds. By the time we were jolting through the lanes to our village, it was all blue; dew still sparkled on the leaves, but the sun was warm. The hills, and the woods, and the shadows in the valleys, looked so extremely beautiful that I had the greatest difficulty in not crying. It was so amazingly clean. The fields of young wheat were a vivid fresh green, the ploughlands a rich chocolate or red, and in between them were the startling yellow squares and rectangles of charlock. I had literally forgotten how bright the English earth could be. In the beech woods strong spikes of deep-blue monkshood pushed their way up through last year's old red leaves.

At the inn everything was clean, there was not a speck of dust. Although it was too warm for a fire a fragrant smell of wood smoke pervaded the whole building, a smell that had no relation to the acrid stench of burning rubble and filthy beams, that had filled my nostrils for months. There was hot water in the bath taps, and the sheets did not stink of plaster dust. A stream frilled with kingcups wriggled across the bottom of the garden and the fat cook's brother caught us two trout for breakfast. It was incredible, and I went to sleep in the sun for four hours.

On the last day of my leave the Germans attacked Russia, and when I got back to our desolate square there was a noticeable rise in people's spirits. Here at last was an ally who would take an active part, not only lease and lend us material, who was well armed and would fight powerfully, not like the gallant but outnumbered

Greeks and Jugoslavs. Despite statements by the 'high-ups' that the Nazis would go through the USSR like a knife through butter, and despite the long retreat, local opinion was confident that the Germans had at last met their match, and that however long it might be, there was now a road that would ultimately lead to victory. In the public bar the situation was sized up: 'I never did believe them Roosians was 'arf as black as they was painted. Seems to me a lot of them is better off than some of us. Here's to 'em, anyway.'

Post 2, Finsbury, after May 10th 1941

'Victory . . . seemed remote and unobtainable . . .'

11

A Worm's-Eye View

As far as one could tell from the worm's-eye view one obtained, the general co-ordinating plans and organisation of London Region worked with remarkable success. Reinforcements to the more heavily hit areas were prompt. People on the spot at an incident would sometimes complain that an ambulance or a stretcher party had been slow in arrival. But it was seldom, in fact, the case. The excitement and sense of urgency of those on the spot made ten minutes seem like half an hour. The system of reports from local Control to Group, and from Group to Region, worked as well as could be expected, allowing for the Luftwaffe's attentions.

It is fair to say that the authorities fell down on at least three major questions—water supply, shelters, and re-housing. In fact, they fell down heavily on these, but by 1941 improvements were made in all of them. There was a great deal of much less publicised work, however, which was admirably controlled. Communications alone, in a place like London, were an enormous problem, and though there was often inevitable confusion during the night, when telephone exchanges were knocked flat, by morning a makeshift scheme was always working. London, of course, is richer, and has more resources than some provincial cities, which were distinctly unhappy in their air-raid precautions when trouble came to them; but at the same time the problems were also greater and more complicated. I do not know how much was due to Admiral Evans and the staff he collected round him, but London Region showed itself resourceful and quick to learn by experience. After the first few incidents, for instance, it was found that the methods that the Heavy Rescue Service had been trained to use were not altogether satisfactory. New methods were devised, and in a very short time indeed Rescue Services all over London received new instructions.

Just before Munich the LCC realised that war was imminent

and that London was totally without defences of any kind. In a frenzy of industry schemes were rushed through, and the only bodies capable of creating the widespread organisation which was needed were the local authorities in each area. When war became a reality the same schemes were implemented. In theory, the choice of the local authority was excellent. Clearly, too much centralisation is dangerous. Had there been, for instance, a few huge rest centres the possibility of colossal disasters would have been increased. But, on the other hand, while some boroughs made fairly adequate provision in this respect, some made hardly any. There was to the end of the war great unevenness. Some areas had their invasion schemes worked out by the beginning of 1942, others still had no such organisation in the spring of 1943.

There are many who hold the view that the Civil Defence services would be far better run, have better discipline, and be more effective if they all came under one national organisation. The running of a service a thousand strong (as one service in one borough is likely to be) is a skilled job, and the type of person who goes in for local government is not, as a rule, capable of it. Officers should receive proper training, and promotions should not be largely dependent on local preferences. When occasionally our local committee did appoint outsiders to jobs, they seemed careless, or perhaps careful, enough to select people no more skilled than themselves for the work. Discipline would have been far easier to maintain if uniform conditions had applied at least all over London.

Some go further and think that the whole of home defence should have been unified—not only casualty services and wardens, but Home Guard, WVS, etc., as well. Allowance could still be made for those who did not wish in any circumstances to be combatants. The work of local national savings groups, housewives' committees, fire-guards, wardens, invasion officers (CD) and Home Guard overlapped. It was frequently the same people who were being called upon in one capacity or the other. Yet there was often very little co-operation between these services. A Post Warden refused to help a member of the WVS who called at his Post to inquire for likely persons in that area, who would be willing to act as savings group organisers. His decision was upheld by his superior officers, on the ground that the WVS was not 'proper Civil Defence,' and its members were not entitled to enter wardens' Posts.

The distinctions between Home Guard and Civil Defence were puzzling. In the early days there was even bad feeling between them. In the provinces wardens were encouraged, sometimes even compelled, to join the Home Guard as well. If there was a raid on they were to act as wardens; if there should have been an invasion they were to have been in the Home Guard. But in London this was not so. When we tried unofficially to get a little Home Guard training from a willing sergeant, it was stopped by our officials, abruptly and categorically. We were told that the reason was that if the Civil Defence personnel had any military training, invading Germans might shoot at them. It is difficult to believe that in the dust and smoke of street battles a Nazi would be even capable, let alone willing, to distinguish between a khaki and a navy blue battle-dress. Any invasion of London would not have been like the occupation of a village, nor would it be like Paris. We were always assured that we would fight for London from every ruin and every pile of débris. In those circumstances nobody was going to be able to stop those of us who wished to, and those who thought that it was worth taking any chance to prevent a Nazi victory, from making use of any weapon that might become available. And in that case one might as well be able to shoot straight.

The demands of industry brought up more important and more conflicting problems. In the present circumstances the country could not afford to have large numbers of men and women standing by idle for an emergency, however likely. On the first call-up for industry from CD personnel, our local authority tried to get rid of the duds—the old and incapable—and those whose opinions they did not like. One can see their intention as regards those in the first category; but if these people were of no use to us, they were not likely to be of much use in a factory, and it was scarcely in the national interest.

By 1943, the call-up had heavily depleted the services, yet we were fairly certain to get more trouble before the war was over. Had there been unified national control, would it not have been possible to organise work of national importance locally? Could not premises have been requisitioned in each area, and the whole Civil Defence personnel employed there, at proper rates, in fairly simple but essential occupations, such as rifle assembly, grenade cases, etc., which do not involve heavy machinery? They would then have remained on the spot and been available, at a few minutes' notice, for raid duties, and at the same time would have been usefully employed, and not stagnating. As it was, those who left went to factories so far away that they could not, however willing, remain on the strength in a voluntary capacity.

It was hardly possible for each local authority to organise such a scheme. It cut across too many departments, ministries and individual interests. I was once told that if I could get sufficient volunteers, stuff could be provided to be made into cordite bags by women wardens on their posts. Within a week there were sufficient volunteers —but we never got the stuff!

What, chiefly, was wrong with the Wardens' Service in Finsbury? (I cannot be sure whether or not these faults characterised other boroughs; but it seems highly probable that some of them at least were to be found in many.) First, the lack of proper treatment of the personnel of the service. Secondly, the appointment of quite unsuitable persons (unsuitable in their qualifications or training, and in their capacity to be natural leaders) to many of the positions at the top of the service locally. Thirdly, discouragement, amounting sometimes to active hostility, of any democratic organisation among the personnel of the service or among the general public.

The wardens' was the ugly duckling of the services, and suffered the most from bad organisation. Ambulance and Heavy Rescue Services came under the LCC and had trained officers appointed by that body, and uniform rules throughout London. Even the casualty services which were controlled locally had, by their nature, to have fully qualified medical officers in charge of them. But the wardens came directly under the local authority, with only circulars from London Region to give guiding rules, which did not always need to be acted upon, and which the personnel seldom saw.

In theory, no doubt this was an excellent arrangement. The warden, more than the Rescue man or the First-Aider, needed to live locally, and to know his fellow-residents. At the beginning of the war a vote was taken as to whether the wardens should come under the local authority or under the police. The borough assured us that we should have a more democratic organisation under it, and won the day easily. In a working-class district the police are not regarded solely as traffic controllers and benign guides for bewildered ladies.

Primarily the wardens were reporting agents, and all the other services depended on the speed and accuracy with which they sent in their reports. But they covered a far wider field than that. They did almost everything, from putting out fires to delivering babies in shelters, from providing general information to rescuing casualties when the débris was not too massive. And the amount of moral support and encouragement that they rendered the public was, in reality, as important as any of these activities. The old people in shelters, of course, thought that anyone who stayed outside was very brave, but for all of them the warden was an assurance that someone cared about them, and that something would be done for them if, and when, they got into trouble. The warden's visit broke the monotony of the long dreary hours in the shelter. He was regarded as a mine of information about everything from relief, re-housing, to the time of the all-clear, and, if there had been one all-clear, whether there would be another alert that night or the next.

It was a very poor warden indeed who did not gain the respect and even affection of the people in his area. The shelterers were seldom so un-English as to express their feelings, but once, when a bomb came down pretty close a minute or so after I had left a shelter, I was astonished to find three of the occupants (who had never been known to leave it from dusk to dawn) running after me to see if I was all right. No doubt part of their action was due to the convention that even in total war it is worse for a woman to get blown up than for a man to meet the same fate. But it made one feel that one's visits to shelters were worth-while. And if that was true in my own case, it was far more true in that of really good wardens like George Palser, who, even before the war, knew every man, woman and child in his street, was always ready to go to great lengths to help them, and was regarded as father and mother and watch-dog combined.

Had the local authority been willing to make a fuller and more proper use of the wardens, much could have been done to improve general conditions, and at the same time to reduce unjustified grumbling. In theory, the wardens were supposed to be the link between the public and the Town Hall, but it remained a theory, and they were often regarded by the latter as even more of a nuisance than the public.

In some boroughs there were wardens' committees which held regular meetings, with officials present, and discussed the various problems. They were started in our district, but, inevitably, lapsed during the raids. Afterwards, when they were restarted and there was a real need for them to hold the service together, their character was changed. For the next year or more, Post Wardens were commanded to attend in the office at rare intervals, and when there, were *told*. No discussion was allowed, and nothing was achieved.

During the raids we were glad enough to be left, as we were, largely to our own devices. In those days we did not have district wardens, and visits from any official were very exceptional. But we became utterly defeatist about any possibility of action being taken on the reports we sent in about damp in shelters, etc. There were also many more personal grievances, such as free bath tickets after raids. It must be remembered that relatively few wardens living east and north of the City had baths in their homes, and a bath after a blitz is essential. We first applied for them in November 1940. We got them (not free, but at a reduced rate) about September 1942. And this was typical of many other complaints which are now old history.

But it was after the raids when the real flaws in the organisation began to show. The Chief Warden's staff in the office increased from three (during the blitz months) to eleven, but without any apparent increase in efficiency. To avoid the charge of inveterate British grumbling, it is worth listing a few of the grievances. If some should appear trivial, it would surely imply that they were all the more avoidable.

We received a flood of circulars almost every week—local versions of London Region's orders. Sometimes we compared them with those that our colleagues in neighbouring boroughs received. They were seldom the same, and generally to our disadvantage. Sometimes they did not even make sense. Civil Defence is not the army. When an order appears to be senseless or unworkable, the average warden or Post Warden considers that he has the right to say so. And unless and until the Government radically changes the basis of Civil Defence, they will probably persist in this idea. On one such occasion, a Post Warden invited a few other Post Wardens to discuss the practicability of one of these orders. A Staff Officer arrived. The Post Warden was degraded to the ranks, and the rest were told that they must not visit other Posts.

When the subsistence voucher was doubled by London Region we did not get the increase until six months after our neighbours. It was argued by some people that the subsistence voucher itself was not really necessary or justified. That was for the Government to decide. But while it existed, it should have been the same for all. It was not going to create a happy or co-operative spirit when voluntary wardens in one borough got half as much in value as their neighbours on the other side of the road, for the same tour of duty, or when full-time male, and part-time male and female wardens, got an allowance, but female full-timers got nothing.

There were perfectly sound rules for taking complaints via the Post Warden to the Chief Warden, and via him to the Controller, and most of us conformed to these, even though the results were meagre, and not infrequently the request for an interview was refused. But the stooges and the tale-bearers did not conform: they went straight to the office, and they *were always granted an interview.* Again, there were several Councillors, both as voluntary and paid wardens, whose chief function, as far as the rest of us could see, seemed to lie in taking ridiculously small matters, which could and should have been settled on the Post, straight to the Emergency Committee.

But our main grievance was the general attitude adopted by the officials to us. When, in the later stages, I had more to do with the Town Hall, I was constantly told by big and small officials, 'Oh, but our wardens are no good. They're a dreadful lot.' Admittedly, we had our 'unreliable characters,' but there are good and bad even in the Navy. And the majority were not only completely honest, but were intelligent, and showed initiative and skill. A good service will never be obtained by reducing everyone to the lowest common denominator. A Post Warden is the equivalent of at least a sergeant in the army. He is directly in charge of twenty to forty people, and responsible for the smooth running of his area, and the efficiency of his Post. If the officers in the army treated their sergeants with the contempt that our Post Wardens received there would be no efficiency in the ranks at all.

They were never consulted. Occasionally they were reprimanded under the notice of the entire strength, and action would be taken on the story of some tale-bearer, without reference being made to them. One or two of them were content to act as martinets and informers for the Town Hall, instead of trying to inculcate a spirit of co-operation and enthusiasm in the Post. But most of them were very bitter about their treatment. Even the part-timers, who did not suffer so much as the paid wardens, did not find many good words to say for the administration. They did not expect to be thanked for any services they might have rendered, but they certainly resented the suggestion that they had remained in the service in order to cadge a uniform, or to dodge fire-watching.

As far as Civil Defence matters were concerned, we did not find the Town Hall exactly efficient. Reports or suggestions seldom received any answer. At a time when it was possible and advisable, at least temporarily, to reserve Post Wardens as key-men, the office concerned neglected to send in the necessary forms.

Another instance sounds scarcely credible. A girl who had been a reliable voluntary warden throughout the raids (she has been mentioned before in these pages) had to leave London soon after they ceased. When she returned she wanted to rejoin. She was already doing fire-watching at her place of work. She wanted to be a voluntary warden as well. The Town Hall sent her to the Labour Exchange, the Labour Exchange sent her back to the Town Hall. Then she was sent to the Labour Exchange in the borough where she worked, from there she was sent to that Town Hall, and from there to the Chief Warden of that area. The Chief Warden said that he could hardly appoint her as a voluntary warden in another borough outside his jurisdiction. All of this took nearly four months, and happened at a time when volunteers were so difficult to get that we were allocated 120 conscripts. A keen volunteer is worth twelve conscripts.

Nor were they very consistent. A Post Warden was discovered to be earning extra money as a fire-watcher. It is clear that it was not possible to be a warden at the same time as being a fire-watcher, who was tied to his building. He was degraded to the ranks. But in two months he was promoted to a higher position than he had held before. Both actions cannot have been right.

The armed services recognise that recreation and sport are necessary. A twelve-hour shift in a warden's Post was probably far more boring, and less healthy, than life in the army usually is. Yet we had the greatest difficulty in getting any such activity going, and only achieved it long after many other boroughs. When we wanted to make a start with a cricket team we received official permission, but no encouragement, of either a financial or any other kind. We were told that it would not work, the wardens were a hopeless lot and would never turn out more than once. True enough, at the first practice only one-third of those who had said they were keen, appeared. But within a month we had a full team and were winning matches, and from the social point of view had an extremely successful season. Wardens from neighbouring Posts, who had barely heard each other's names before, now met for the first time, and a really friendly team came into being. But we could not help noticing the difference when we visited other boroughs, and found that the Chief Warden or a Staff Officer came out to greet us, and that the other team had been given a grant or a donation with which to purchase their gear. Members of our team subscribed 3d. or 6d. per match, and persuaded some of our friends or onlookers to do the same if we could. It was good exercise, but more important —it drew members of different Posts and services together.

This however, seemed to be precisely what the Town Hall did not like. Had they been able (and willing) to organise such activities themselves and hand them out on a plate, like charity from a beneficent higher being, maybe they would have shown less hostility. But the moment any committee was formed of the men themselves they seemed to fear that it would become a breeding-ground for sedition. There is nothing like putting ideas into people's heads.

Discussion groups were started on the lines, and only on the subjects, suggested by the LCC and London Region. As they were beginning to gain support the Emergency Committee passed a resolution that they could not be held on premises belonging to the Council, unless and until the EC could consider the subjects for discussion. The usual excuse was produced—that the groups were the work of conscientious objectors and communists. It is hardly surprising that many analogies began to be drawn between the local and the Nazi régimes.

All this did not make for a spirit of willingness, and as a result discipline was far slacker than it should have been. The wardens were discontented, but almost the only retort possible was to abstain from turning out on official parades in their off-time, which was not very effective, and in any case they were then commanded to do so.

The men in the casualty and Rescue Services worked and had their recreation as a group in their depots. But the wardens were split up into small Posts, and while the official attitude was to keep them separate, they seldom had a chance to meet each other. There was the trade union branch, but there were usually so many actual grievances on the agenda that there was little time for more informal discussion, or for social activity. Officially, the Town Hall approved of people becoming members of the union. But, when a resolution was passed which was not to their taste, they found means of discharging the chairman and other active members.

More than a year after the lull had started a social club was formed. It had a bitter struggle for existence at first. There was the apathy caused by three years of neglect to overcome, and again the main official objection seemed to be to the committee which was, for the first time, composed of delegates from each Post and depot. There is some value in exercise and amusement for its own sake, but much more if it is, as far as is possible within service rules, self-governed and organised by the personnel themselves.

National organisation and appointment of efficient officers would have removed some of these anomalies and grievances. But it would still have been only half the battle. Had the wardens, for instance, come under the police, there might have been a more efficient organisation technically, but they would probably have lost that friendly relationship with the public which was their chief asset. What is most essential in home defence is truly democratic organisation. In the army it is now realised that a Tennysonian attitude of not reasoning why will not win a modern war, even if it could be obtained and enforced on a sufficiently wide scale. Still less is such an attitude obtainable among the ordinary public—without the regimentation of the fascist system. The Germans—or most of them—had dinned into them a fanatical faith in their system. We—or most of us—believe in democracy. But the democratic ideal has been degraded only to its negative aspect. Far too many people think that democracy means the maximum of non-interference by the State in their affairs, instead of the maximum interest and interference by them in State affairs.

During the period of continuous raiding there was an admirable opportunity for building up an active democratic faith. People came out of the obscurantist isolation of their homes, and together they became braver and less selfish. The more energetic became shelter marshals and wardens. A local council is elected to represent the people. What was needed was real co-operation between them all—committees of the shelterers themselves with their marshal, of wardens' representatives and those of the local administration. Democracy is more trouble to organise and more cumbrous than the totalitarian system. And it is easy to rail at the delays and stupidities of committees, but they are the only guarantee against fascism abroad and at home. In the boroughs where such committees were formed they had considerable success.

A Labour Council should be the ideal body to accomplish this organisation, provided that the councillors maintain the socialist principle that they represent the people and are responsible to them, and do not set out to become tin-pot officials and rulers in their own personal right.

If a local authority really represents, leads and services its people, there can be no more suitable body to direct affairs. But there were far too many councillors who heaved a sigh of relief when local elections were stopped, and thought that it absolved them from doing anything, or who thought it an excellent opportunity to acquire more personal power, and become local tin gods. Ours was not the only borough where mayors, for instance, were made Chief Warden, whether they had any experience or talent for the work or not. Even in peace-time a mayor has a full engagement list; in war he has many more commitments. He cannot have the time to run a service of a thousand men and women. It is by no means an easy job and requires training, or at least great aptitude.

Ours was a Labour borough, and before the war had a good record in re-housing, public health, etc. When the blitzes started we had high expectations of it, and the provision of a large number of shelters encouraged those expectations. But as the war developed the local leaders seemed to lose all realisation that they were responsible for and *to* the population, that they were servants as well as rulers. More and more it seemed to become a matter of a small group of leaders—a caucus—striving to run everything and to keep most jobs and appointments in their own hands. They co-operated with London Region as little as possible on the grounds that they could run things better themselves. At the same time they allowed the local Labour Party (which had, after all, elected them to their positions) to fall into complete decay. No meetings were held, dues were not paid, the premises were deserted.

When there were vacancies on the Council these seemed to be

filled by carefully selected stooges who could be relied on to vote the right way when told, and who had little or no record of having taken any interest in public welfare. There was no meeting of the Labour Party, or of Union branches affiliated to it, to discuss the candidates. There was, so we were told, a Trades Council. But it only existed on paper. And its paper existence was used, more than once, to stop the formation of a real one. The Labour Party also ceased to be anything more than a notepaper heading. When there is no contact between the electors and elected, no vitality in the Party organisation which is in power, the original conception of local government becomes at best bureaucracy, and at its worst a not incorruptible tyranny.

Briefly, what was needed? What, positively could have been done other than what was done? In the first place, a properly functioning Labour Party and a Trades Council, voicing needs and grievances from the wards, or branches, or places of work, criticising and checking the red tape and ineptitude where these occurred, and, above all, insisting on the treatment of people *as people*, could have made a great deal of difference. They would have been the nucleus of a live local leadership, as well as providing a forum for discussion (and out of discussion, understanding of the political implication of events which was so much needed). It could have helped to break down sectionalism, and to check the tendency for an official caucus to centralise appointments in the hands of a small, charmed circle and its nominees, and could have helped in promoting those with a talent for leadership, and for winning trust and affection.

Secondly, a proper democratic organisation within the Wardens' Service itself (and in the other Civil Defence Services also) could have rectified many mistakes, as well as developing an atmosphere of willing co-operation, and individual responsibility and initiative, in place of the sour grumbling and 'browned off' feeling that became only too common. Regular wardens' meetings, and committees of wardens in a particular area (possibly joint committees of several CD services), could have handled, not only matters of service routine, but also educational and recreational activities, welfare—even, to a certain extent, shelter welfare—all of which, in the circumstances, tended to be neglected.

Thirdly, the encouragement at an early date of shelter committees and elected shelter marshals, acting in the closest co-operation with the wardens, might not only have secured a quicker remedy for many of the grievances that have been referred to above, but would have developed a community feeling among the shelterers, and a sense of responsibility in guiding their own destinies. It would have made all the difference in those long months of nightly bombardment. As it was, they were allowed very tardily, and extremely half-heartedly, when most of the raiding was over.

That, in the absence of these things, the ordinary people of London showed the stubborn fortitude they did, for so long, is something of a miracle. I think that their existence, in combination, would have made all the difference between what was often a blind and uncomprehending stubbornness, and the steeled heroism of free men and women who know they are in the fight, and why: that a new spirit could have been forged which would have transformed London, and been a shining beacon in those post-Dunkirk days when hope burned very low indeed.

Properly trained officers to run the services from the technical point of view were needed, but a true democratic basis in the locality was a far more fundamental necessity. No one was in as close touch with the ordinary people as the warden. He often had more sway than columns of propaganda in the newspapers, or posters on the hoardings. Our local authority feared the 'voice of the people,' and even more, they disliked the voice of the warden. Home defence is not merely a technical business. The citizen being bombed needs to have more faith in the nation's cause than the soldier. Let no one think that because of press phrases about 'taking it,' and much-quoted Cockney jokes while bricks and mortar were crashing to rubble, that there were not many who groaned every time that we raided Germany, in dread of the retaliation that they would get.

It was the lack of a clear and positive ideal, as much as the lack of armaments, that made the dark days of 1939-41 so very dark. The destruction of one man and his group of henchmen alone could scarcely justify a war in which millions are to be killed. It is the destruction of a vile and sub-human system that can be the only justification. And for that, understanding, not slavish acquiescence, is needed. We were fighting for democracy—the only way to do that thoroughly is to understand it, and to understand it one must be able to see evidence of it in every walk of life, in factories, in shelters, in CD services, and in the local government itself.

12

Postcript

The last major raid of the blitz on London came on May 10th, 1941. Although we did not know it, there were to be no more devastating attacks on London for almost three years. The tasks of clearing and tidying after the devastation went on, but there was no guaranteeing that any rebuilding would not immediately be destroyed once more. Most industrial resources were, moreover, devoted entirely to the production of war materials. There was a lull, a time when one went about one's daily business with a certain watchfulness, waiting to see what would happen next.

There is always a degree of inactivity in waiting and life at an ARP post was no exception. It was boring and I felt less useful, so I decided to end my full-time employment as a warden. I took a couple of so-called 'exams' and became an ARP instructor, reverting to being a voluntary warden on night duty. It was during this period that I wrote *Raiders Overhead*. For anyone who lived through it, the experience of the blitz was unforgettable, but, for something to do and also to preserve the detail of what went on, I wrote it down.

I had also formed strong views about the way in which the Civil Defence services, and the Wardens' Service in particular, were organised, and expressed them in the last chapter of the book. Whether or not anyone with any power to reorganise the Service read them I do not know. The book came out in 1943, and in the spring of 1944 we were once more defending ourselves against attack from the air.

This time the threat came not from the massed heavy bombers of the Luftwaffe, but from the new-fangled 'flying bomb'. The first one landed, I believe, near Bow Bridge. All sorts of rumours sprang up: 'the priest had been blown to bits, no trace of him left'; 'the pilot had baled out over Surrey – the dirty dog.' The first night provided a spectacular display. I have never seen anything to equal it: all the guns in Kent and Surrey opened up, the Home Guard in Hyde Park and other open spaces followed with their 'drain-pipes', which exploded at a given height releasing showers of lesser containers full of explosive. Our own local gun emerged from its bit of tunnel on the only north-south bit of railway line in London from King's Cross to Farringdon Street, where it lay hidden by day, and let off its salvoes literally alongside our feet. Still one bomb buzzed on, emitting its trail of flames and smoke, till it got to Hampstead Hill where it ran out of fuel and came down in the open doing no serious damage.

On the whole we did not mind the flying bombs so much as the HE. Night or day you could usually see them coming, and hear the cut-out just before it dropped. If you lay flat on the ground you were probably safe at even only six or seven yards. They all had an impact fuse, and therefore although they blew in countless facades or backs of buildings, they did not bring down whole edifices. There were of course unlucky exceptions. One cut-out over the river, just cleared Bush House and fell in the Aldwych just as the streets were full of office workers hurrying to try to get some lunch. One of our wardens who worked in the area got caught in that one and was taken to hospital. He returned to our post in the evening after they had extracted the object which had been blown into his leg – it was a button.

Another fell in the central courtyard of the Royal Free Hospital. This was a couple of hundred yards off my area – but a hospital, I felt, justified straying off one's beat. When I got there I found that it had been decided to evacuate the entire hospital. The structure had not been so very badly damaged, but all the doors and windows had gone and the lifts were out of action. I grabbed a stretcher and helped to bring four or five patients down. The last one in that ward was already lying on his face on a stretcher – but a hospital stretcher with two-inch by two-inch wooden handles, not like ours of light tubular metal, and the nurses said he must not be jiggled or joggled as he was a bad thrombosis case. He also had large pieces of the window glass sticking into his back. Unluckily I got the head end, and had to come down the stairs in a squatting, crab-like position sticking my legs out sideways like a Cossack dancer.

Eventually we got him down to the street. There was a line of ambulances waiting, but the monstrous stretcher was too long for the Civil Defence ambulance. Fortunately an American Red Cross van drew up. We got him in, but the doctor insisted that he and I should go in it. I said, 'Oh no, I'm not First Aid, I'm Warden's Service', but he persisted, so I did. The van started off at a rate of knots – potholes and all. Rashly I suggested that we ought to take the strain, so we squatted on our heels each side and held the stretcher to reduce the jolting.

All the way the man kept making awful gurgling noises. When we got to Barts, the American vehicle was too big to get through the gate. 'Never mind,' said the doctor, 'we'll carry him. It's only seventy or eighty yards'. Only! My shoulders already felt as though my arms were leaving their sockets. But off we went and with every step I became more and more convinced that I should drop my end. When we set him down on the casualty reception floor, I grabbed the first nurse to pass, and rather gasped. 'Is this one still alive?' She said yes, so I seized another light stretcher and hurried off. A bus went a bit of the way, but I had no money on me. 'Never you mind, ducks, you have it on the firm', said the conductor, and I arrived back in my post to be ticked off by my Post Warden for leaving my area.

Soon after this I was translated to higher things, became a lecturer, and officially organising secretary, at headquarters of London Region in Kensington. Lectures were to senior members of CD, Chief Wardens, Fire Service and American personnel destined for the continent. One lecture was enlivened by a bomb exploding not far down the road from the building where we were. The incident provided a first-class opportunity for the 'students', in this case American troops, to see the Civil Defence forces in action at first hand. They put on a good show and the Americans were, I believe, duly impressed. There was even a lecture given on decontamination of corpses in the event of gas. This was a rather ghoulish affair given to forty morticians, and it was made more dreadful by the sight of a rather weedy little man with a draggled moustache and a wide gap between his front teeth into which he inserted a cigarette, which hung there till only ash was left, while he sat in the front row with mouth wide open and goggling eyes.

At long last, D-Day arrived. Not for five years had we heard any aircraft overhead in London except enemy ones and now, wave after wave of our own planes thundered and roared above us. What an invigorating sound: people stood in the street and cheered, though many were apprehensive who had sons or husbands taking part in the invasion.

Of course, the fly-bombs went on. Perhaps they even increased in numbers. They were augmented by V-2s, rocket bombs of great size (45 feet long and weighing 14 tons) which travelled so high and so fast that one had no sound or warning until they exploded and caused extremely widespread damage. Nevertheless their direction-finding apparatus was not very accurate, and while Ilford and the lower marshy regions of the Thames got a great many, central London only had eight. But those eight made some horribly big gaps in the much scarred capital. Before the Nazis had managed to improve their design, Allied troops had battled their way through Caen, and, after heavy fighting, eventually reached the launching pads in the Pas de Calais and silenced them. There was still a long hard way to battle on the continent on both western and eastern fronts, but London itself had relative peace.

At last on May 8th, 1945 came VE-Day. In the evening I called on my Post Warden. We decided to go out for a bit of a pub crawl. But pub after pub was closed: 'no beer' was chalked on their doors. We managed to find a pint or two at last, but it seemed that all the beer supplies had been sent to the West End. We went back to his house, which, though it had no windows, was still standing, and he found some whisky. When I left, I turned on the doorstep, and said, 'Now mind, after all this, that you don't fall over in front of a bus', and promptly disappeared down an old bomb hole just in front of his house.

Like all the other services, the CD forces were demobilised after the war. There was not much in the way of thanks, but then one didn't expect it – that was not the reason for having volunteered in the first place. I stayed in London for another five or six years, earning my living in the still infant television industry and trying to perform some service to the borough. One of the principal needs, after the devastation of the bombing, was the reconstruction of people's homes, and an enormous amount was achieved under circumstances of great scarcity of money and materials.

No amount of money could restore the borough to its former state and, considering the conditions in which many people lived before the war, that was probably no bad thing. On the other hand, the new estates, the architect-designed flats, the attempts at spacious gardens have thrown up different problems. And the spirit of community fostered by the common threat of destruction from the air fairly quickly subsided as old habits reasserted themselves. While they were in the skies, or threatened to return, the raiders overhead were a terrifying symptom of the changing scale of power at man's command, but the fact that neither the German bombers, nor the Allied destroyers of German cities, put an end to the resistance of the people attacked shows even more clearly that life goes on under the most intense and fearful pressure, and that it is all but impossible to destroy the will to live.

Acknowledgements

Picture credits

BBC Hulton Picture Library: 14–15, 19, 21, 24, 33, 47, 51, 73, 80–1,
104–5, 107, 115, 137, 143, 145, 157
Ferens Art Gallery, Hull: 77
Imperial War Museum: 40 (top), 52, 57, 61
London Fire Brigade: 28–9, 111, 113, 117, 140–1, 151
London Transport Executive: 40 (bottom), 59
Ramsey & Muspratt: 2
Crown Copyright: 156

Cover photograph: Michael Busselle

The publishers are grateful to Letchworth Museum Services and Nicholas
Maddren for the loan of items used in the cover photograph.

The text of *Raiders Overhead* was first published by
Lindsay Drummond Ltd in 1943. This revised and
enlarged edition first published by Scolar Press and
Gulliver Publishing Co in 1980.
Unless otherwise stated, the line drawings in the text are by
Barbara Nixon.